South-East Ireland

Heaven on Earth

To all my family

Heaven on Earth

The characters, eccentrics and experiences growing up in the bottom right-hand corner of the Emerald Isle

Patrick Donegall

NINE ELMS BOOKS

Published in 2023 by
Nine Elms Books
Unit 1g, Clapham North Arts Centre
26-32 Voltaire Road,
London SW4 6DH
info@nineelmsbooks.co.uk
www.nineelmsbooks.co.uk

ISBN print 978-1-910533-76-5

Copyright © 2023 Patrick Donegall

Protected by copyright under the terms of the International Copyright Union.
The rights of Patrick Donegall to be identified as the author of this work have been asserted by him in accordance with
the Copyright, Designs and Patents Act, 1988. All rights reserved.

This book is sold under the condition that no part of it may be reproduced, copied, stored in a retrieval system or transmitted in any form
or by any means, electronic, mechanical, photocopying, recording or otherwise without prior – permission of the author.

Every effort has been made to contact all copyright holders. The publishers will be pleased to amend in future editions
any errors or omissions brought to their attention.

Cover illustrations and cartoons by Oliver Preston.
Cover design, text design, typesetting, end papers and layout by Simon French.

All photographs are from the author's private family collection except those kindly provided by the Marquess of Waterford,
Julie Berridge, Charles Green, Jessica Harrington, Mark & Emma Hewlett, Harry McCalmont and Pat McCalmont.

Printed and bound in India

CONTENTS

Acknowledgements 1

Preface 5

Dunbrody Park 7

Killesk Church and the Clergy 13

The Pony Club and learning to ride 21

Hunting in Wexford and Kilkenny 31

Mount Juliet 47

Costello and other fishing stories 59

Snipe shooting in the wilderness 73

Other characters 83

The south east and its treasurers 95

Words of caution 107

Hope for the future 109

Epilogue 119

ACKNOWLEDGEMENTS

So many people have helped me with the production of this book, that I am afraid I may have left someone out. I do hope not.

The people I mention here I have thanked in no particular order. They were all supportive, and they all encouraged me to pursue this project. I hope they will feel that their cooperation has been worthwhile.

Since so much of this book is devoted to the world of the horse and its place in the life of the South East of Ireland, it makes sense to start there.

Jessie Harrington's great success in the world of National Hunt racing, and now on the flat, is recorded. She is my late sister's sister-in-law and helped with the provision of some wonderful photographs. When I picked them up, I was treated to the spectacle of some of her 200-odd horses in training doing their stuff on the gallops. For those who have never seen a major racing stable in action, it can only be described as a military operation.

Harry McCalmont's contribution was terrific. He checked the chapter on Mount Juliet, and passed it as a true reflection on life there in the time of his father and grandfather. Also, Pat McCalmont for providing the picture of his father and mother without which this book would be incomplete. Moving on I should like to thank the Berridge and Lambert families. They again produced wonderful photographs and many amusing (I hope) anecdotes. I would make a special mention of Charlie and Jenny Berridge, who consented to the use of an unusual and not entirely flattering photograph of them with the wonderful Boodie Cairns. Patrick Lambert cleared up a number of issues and corrected details that I would otherwise have got wrong.

Johnny Price, in his inimitable style, was very illuminating as far as the goings-on at Kilmokea were concerned. I should also like to thank Mark and Emma Hewlett, who succeeded the Price family, for their photographs of the house and garden.

The Marquess of Waterford (Tyronie) gave me such help by allowing access to the albums at Curraghmore. These really are a hidden gem, and record a life in Ireland that has almost vanished. Many thanks to his first cousin, Sir Francis Brooke, for allowing the photograph of his parents' wedding. I have a feeling this was my first appearance in public, and I did not behave well! Francis is now the King's representative at Ascot.

The Hon. Gerald Maitland-Carew (always known as Bunny) provided all the anecdotes to do with Castletown and the Kildare Hunt. He provided so many good stories that I have not found room for them all. Bunny was a Cavalry offiicer, and so was Sir Michael Strang Steel, who, as an ex-Adjutant of the 17th/21st Lancers, gave his expert opinion on the validity of the orders which Uncle Ken Alexander was issuing from his bed in Milford. It seems to me that had Uncle Ken actually issued those orders to the 17th Lancers at Balaclava, then the Charge of the Light Brigade would never have taken place. The reason being that his orders would have made no sense to anyone.

Charles Verschoyle-Greene who lives at Milford, the stamping ground of the Alexanders, produced stories and photographs galore. I knew most of the stories, but had none of the photographic evidence. His pictures of Mrs. Hall confirm that she was unique – the sort of woman who does not exist today.

Simon Conyngham, originally from Slane Castle, provided the majority of the accounts of the revelries at Costello. Illegal drinking and eels in the bath were not the half of it.

I would like to thank P.J.Gibbons, the editor and publisher of Social & Personal magazine, who approved the inclusion of Desmond and Ollie Lambert's wedding photograph. The magazine flourishes to this day. Also, many of the early hunting photographs have been reproduced with the permission of Jim Meads who took them. He is long retired and lives in Wales, but is in good spirits.

There needs to be a particular thank you to Oliver Preston who found time to do the cartoons. His cartoons are well known and apart from in Country Life, he has had work published in The Field, the Spectator, and many other titles.

Finally, what would I have done without Diana Beasley who corrected my dreadful grammar and punctuation, and all the team at Richard Greenlys, who worked wonders improving and restoring some very dilapidated photographs. Last but not least – a word for my wife Caroline and daughter Katie who have had to put up with my struggles in the last year to get this to the publishers. Hugh Williams, who has taken on this chore, and Simon French who has wrestled with the graphic design, have had derisory help from the author. Both of them deserve a medal. Sir Anthony Weldon who I knew slightly from my army days has taken over the publishing duties at a later stage. His advice has proved invaluable.

PREFACE

Sometime, just before she died, my older sister Chich Fowler was asked, by an English friend, what it was like growing up in the South East of Ireland in the 1950s and 1960s.

Her reply was very succinct. "Heaven on Earth" was her description. While that might be overdoing it a touch, it was certainly the most wonderful stage for those of a sporting inclination, and for those whose natural home was a rural wilderness. Most of the characters in this book were willing actors on that stage, and their refusal to take life or themselves too seriously shines through.

For the purposes of this book, I include in the South East of Ireland the counties Wexford, Waterford, Kilkenny, and Carlow. As far as the world of Irish tourism was concerned, those counties hardly featured. Anyone who went into a Failte Ireland office in, say, London, would be directed to Dublin, or more likely the western counties of Cork, Kerry and Galway. What a treat they were missing! The South East of the country is a hidden gem indeed. It is different now but in the days of my youth no-one in authority cared about this part of Ireland.

The actors on this stage had the place to themselves. The tourism industry which has brought so much prosperity to rural Ireland was still a gleam in some tourist board official's eye. It was then, and to a lesser extent is now, a sporting paradise. It boasted the best of horses, the best of fishing, the best of rough, particularly snipe, shooting, and the best of craic. Taking part in this world were some very improbable characters indeed. I arrived on this scene in May 1952.

My father had inherited Dunbrody Park and the Cistercian Abbey of Dunbrody in Wexford from his father in the late 1940s, shortly after the end of the Second World War, most of which he had spent as a guest of Mr. Hitler.

He and my mother were determined to make the most of their good fortune, and got involved in all that the South East had to offer. As children we did not know how lucky we were.

While this book will on occasion report on escapades in Dublin, Galway and other parts of Ireland, it is primarily about the thrills and spills of growing up in the bottom right-hand corner of the Emerald Isle. It is about the characters who made it what it was, and the scrapes they got into.

It may seem unlikely, but everything in this book is based on fact. None of it is pure fiction. Some slight embellishment maybe, but all of it is based on the truth, and the names in the book have not been changed. This may have been the last hoorah of the ascendancy, but what a way to go!

CHAPTER ONE

Dunbrody Park

Dunbrody Park was where I grew up. While it was my childhood home, I am lucky enough to spend about half the year there to this day.

To give a few historical facts, the house was built by Lord Spencer Stanley Chichester 1775-1819 who was the 3rd son of Arthur Chichester, the 1st Marquess of Donegall. It was Spencer's son Arthur who as a politician of some note was created the 1st Lord Templemore. He lived from 1797 to 1837 which was another short innings. The title Templemore thus became a minor Chichester title, and it was not till 1975 that the title of Marquess of Donegall was reunited with the Wexford property. That was the year that the 6th Marquess died and was succeeded by my father. Enough of that.

Spencer Chichester created a sizeable and comfortable country house, which was completed about 1810, and it was this that my parents moved to in 1950. Its location is part of its charm. The whole property is perched up on a cliff overlooking Waterford harbour, and every day you can get a bird's eye view of ships making their way up river to Belview Port which is just a few miles from Waterford city. Waterford harbour is a bit of a misnomer in that it extends some 12 miles from the city to the open sea by the Hook lighthouse. The estuary opposite Dunbrody Park is some 2 to 3 miles across to the Waterford side. Quite a harbour.

The house itself, like so many, has had a chequered history. During my grandfather's time it was only visited in the summer, and was left to the staff to do as they please in the other months. One of the staff that I remember was a remarkable character called William Lambert who masqueraded as a butler. He was not only English but a Protestant and infrequently sober. On one occasion around 1920, the local IRA came to call with the intention of doing away with Lambert and torching the house. Lambert, who was much the worse for wear, took aim with an ancient blunderbuss from an upper window, and only succeeded in blowing off part of the roof. The IRA left in confusion.

William Lambert was inherited by my parents along with the house, whether they liked it or not, which they probably didn't. His sole duties seemed to be twofold. First to collect the post from the village and second to polish my father and mother's hunting boots. Neither task did he excel at.

As far as the post was concerned, this was normally collected after a prolonged stay in the Kings Bay Inn. The inevitable consequence was that most of the post was mislaid on the hill up from Arthurstown. On one occasion my father was accosted by Matt Foley the local butcher demanding that his long overdue bill should be paid.

"But you have never sent me a bill," said my father. "Nonsense", said Matt, "I have sent you four." On investigation all the bills and others were found in the gutter above the village. Lambert was just one of the personalities at Dunbrody in my childhood. Another was the governess that my parents engaged, the formidable Miss Paskins. She was in fact a very good, methodical teacher. The reader might query that after reading this book, but she did manage to get me and my two sisters into good schools in England.

Miss Paskins, or Passy as we knew her, amused my parents by always referring to her one fat leg. My father, rather uncharitably, always said that both legs looked equally fat to him. She taught a lot of the young from Irish country houses. How she retained her sanity remains a mystery.

Mary Cahill was the housekeeper. She was a domestic servant of the kind who would always be seen enthusiastically sweeping up the dust in one corner of the room, and surreptitiously sweeping it under the carpet in the other.

A marvellous old lady, she was totally bald, but with a long flowing beard. My mother was transfixed one day when she miscued, when lighting one of her Capstan Full Strength, and set fire to her beard, thereby levelling things up with the top of her head.

The farm at Dunbrody along with a smaller one at Dunbrody Abbey, three miles away, was run by the steward, Peter Murphy. Mr. Murphy had under his command a fairly motley crew, but he did have in Peter and Willie Cummins two highly skilled carpenters. They built an enormous dolls house for my elder sister, which was modelled on the castle at Dunbrody Abbey, and is on display there to this day.

It would not be fair to level too much by way of criticism at Peter Murphy for the way the farm was run, and therefore the lack of profit. The whole operation was conducted in order to facilitate my parents' enthusiasm for hunting. The horses and their stabling ruled supreme. Conventional farming activities came a poor second. Did I complain about this? Certainly not – I was a willing accomplice.

One of the new-fangled contraptions for most of that part of the world was the telephone. Our telephone number in Dunbrody Park was Duncannon 4, the first three Duncannon numbers being the lighthouse, the Garda station, and the hotel. On one memorable occasion my mother was discussing with a friend whether they should visit an elderly lady in the neighbourhood who had been poorly.

All of a sudden, a third voice joined the conversation with the following advice: "There is no point going to see Mrs. Doyle. She is not there. She has been taken to Hospital." No harm in a bit of casual eavesdropping I suppose. Even so it rather shocked my mother.

Overseeing all this activity was a firm called EMSA who specialised in managing old family estates. We had two EMSA representatives when I was young. The first was a delightful man called Jodie Carey, who had been a prisoner of the Japanese and was

Self as a young officer in the Coldstream Guards. The complete absence of any kind of medal is a fair reflection of my contribution to the military machine of the 1970s. I adored the Coldstream Guards – A wonderful Regiment.

worked nearly to death on the Burma railway. Jodie was a very keen philatelist, and got me interested in stamp collecting, an interest I have to this day. He helped me to start a collection. He did have one golden rule. Under no circumstances was I to include a Japanese stamp in the collection. I broke the rule once with a rather attractive issue from the Land of the Rising Sun. Jodie spotted it and tore it into little pieces, accompanied by a lot of finger wagging.

The second agent was a man called Peter de Stacpoole, from County Meath. Also a delightful man, he had to contend with my father as he got older, and, as the Irish would put it, more contrary.

One of the great occasions at Dunbrody Park took place in 1971 when my sister Jenny, always known as Chich, married John Fowler of Rahinston also in County Meath. John was a famous amateur jockey and was the brother of Jessie Harrington of Moscow Flyer and Sizing John fame, to name but two of her many winners.

Sadly, I was not even present at the time. I had just joined the Army and on the day of the wedding was on exercise with the Coldstream Guards, on the North German plain. I seem to remember causing mayhem on an Autobahn at round about the time they went up the aisle. For all the impact I had on the Cold War, I might as well have been at the wedding.

By all accounts it was a great occasion, enjoyed by all in true Irish style, to the extent that one man was found the following day asleep in a flower bed with his arms folded over his chest and a bunch of flowers tastefully arranged to keep him company. The beatific smile on his face suggested that all was well with his world.

Julie, my younger sister, married Andrew Frazer from Culleybackey, County Antrim, some 10 years later. At her wedding my father had failed to check on the condition of the marquee beforehand. It had obviously been used at some agricultural show last time out, and was covered in cow dung. A friend from England was delighted to hear my father, who was by then a Marquess, say to no-one in particular, "I don't know which Marquee is in more trouble – this one or that one." Pointing at the tent.

This was the happy family home I grew up in, though it could be said that my attempts at growing up were not always successful. I will be eternally grateful to my parents for such a start.

The wedding of Sir George Brooke Bt. and Lady Melissa Wyndham-Quinn. This took place at Adare Manor in Limerick. I am second from the Left. On my right is Lord Valentine Cecil. To my left is my great friend from Harrow and the army, Neil McCorquodale, and on his left is Harry McCalmont, who helped so much with this book.

CHAPTER TWO

Killesk Church and the Clergy

My parents were very devout churchgoers. My father had been baptised into the Church of Ireland, and my mother, who came from a similar background, was of the same persuasion. While they were loyal Protestants, they were neither of them in any way bigoted. They both recognized the need to respect the traditions and practices of other religions. Living where they did for nigh on fifty years, this meant getting along with the huge Roman Catholic majority.

I would hesitate to put a figure on it, but at a guess the population of that part of Ireland might have been 95% Catholic, 5% Protestant. In these more secular days, and with many other religions such as Muslim and Hindu represented, those figures might be a bit different, probably much lower.

We were lucky, living at Dunbrody Park, in the sense that the local church had been built by the family, for the family. It was situated on land donated by them just opposite the gates of the back drive. Called All Saints Killesk, it is a charming small church, with seating for maybe 60 to 70 worshippers. It was built in 1877 and was opened a year later, and paid for entirely by subscription with no church or state funds involved. As such it was a genuinely private church.

The fund-raising was organized entirely by my great-great-grandfather, Harry Spencer Chichester, the 2nd Lord Templemore, 1821-1906. The way he did it was extraordinary. He was an enthusiastic member of the House of Lords, and in regular attendance when the House was sitting. As a result, he came into contact with, and befriended, a large number of the most influential people in these islands.

These were the people who paid for the construction of All Saints Killesk. Many of them had no connection with Ireland whatsoever. I imagine there was a rush for the door when Harry Chichester appeared with his hat held out! I still have the subscription list in the family papers. In their ranks were the following, to name but a few: The Duke of Marlborough, who contributed five pounds, the Earl of Glasgow – three guineas, and the Dowager Marchioness of Cholmondeley – also five pounds. As far as I know, none of these owned Irish properties, or were involved with the country in any way.

The largest contribution, appropriately enough, was Lord Templemore who chipped in 122 pounds 5 shillings and 9 pence. In joint last place were the Reverend Cope, and a Mr. Russell, both of whom produced half a crown. Still, it's the thought that counts. It is a fascinating social commentary on the times. It is hard to visualize anybody having a whip-round to build a church today.

The total sum raised was 1486 pounds 5 shillings and a penny. This was a substantial sum and proved more than adequate to produce a fine building. It has particularly impressive stained-glass windows. These all date to 1877 with one exception. A recent addition was erected in memory of my mother who died in 1995.

This was the church which we were expected to attend every Sunday, come rain or shine. My father always read the lesson, would have no truck with the modern prayer book, and, as far as offering a "sign of peace" was concerned, he simply refused to take part. In short, he did not approve of trendy, happy-clappy vicars. The traditional church service was fine by him, with no alterations required.

We had a diverse collection of rectors of the New Ross and Fethard Union. In those days the Rector was responsible for all six churches in the Union – New Ross, Fethard, Old Ross, Whitechurch, Tintern, and Killesk. This meant that the poor man had his hands full. It also meant he had a big mileage to cover since there were services in most of the churches every Sunday. I am not sure how they managed it.

The first rector I remember was the Reverend Adrian Fisher. Mr. Fisher had been a chaplain in the RAF, and was a nice enough man. However, it would be fair to say that he was not the sharpest tool in the box. He always found preaching a sermon something of an ordeal, as did the congregation who had to listen to it. Put simply, he could never think of anything to say. On one occasion he spoke for just under two minutes, which was short by any standard. My father, who did not approve of long sermons, and would start tapping his watch after 10 minutes, was absolutely delighted. "Just the right length," said my father, "It was rubbish anyway."

The Fishers asked my parents to lunch in the Rectory in Fethard. According to my mother, things were going just fine, and they had worked their way through a bowl of nondescript soup. Pam Fisher swept up the bowls and went into the kitchen to get the main course – roast chicken with all the trimmings.

Adrian and Pam had, at the time, an ancient and malevolent looking lurcher, and it was this hound that Pam tripped over, when carrying most of the main course. The lurcher needed no invitation and made off with the

All Saints Killesk – My family church which was built by subscription by my great-great-grandfather.

chicken in a hurry. Pam reappeared covered in gravy and bread sauce in floods of tears. Adrian's response was as follows: "But, darling, you look so gorgeous, doesn't she?" My father muttered, sotto voce I hope, that that was a matter of opinion.

My mother said later that the vegetables on their own were really quite pleasant. My father replied that he was not a vegetarian and had no intention of becoming one. Party of the year? Perhaps not.

The next incumbent was the Reverend Teevan Armstrong. Teevan was a charming if rather unworldly person. He was a thoroughly good man.

My parents' graves. They have an idyllic resting place overlooking the estuary of the three rivers, the Nore, Suir, and Barrow

Unlike some of his calling he clearly believed in God – a good start. He did have one major handicap. He was almost completely blind.

Mercifully in the 1960s, in that part of the world, the traffic was very sparse. A certain amount of it had four legs rather than four wheels. Nevertheless, Teevan on his dilapidated scooter was a very considerable threat to other road users. He certainly caused one road accident and probably more. Things would have been better if it had been the law in Ireland to drive on the right-hand side of the road, which Teevan tended to do. Unfortunately, that was not the case.

I can remember him losing his glasses one Sunday, which meant that he got lost on the way to the pulpit from the altar. He actually went into the vestry and he had to be assisted into the pulpit by my father. I inspected the missing glasses once, and the lenses were as thick as the bottom of a champagne bottle.

It was during Teevan's time that the problem of the ancient harmonium, and who was to play it, came to the fore. The practical solution for Killesk Church was to invest in a gramophone with a modest library of pre-recorded hymns. If my memory serves me well, "Abide with me" got an airing every other Sunday. All was fine while my mother was in charge. She made it her business to man the contraption. Things went wrong when my mother was away one Sunday, and my sister Chich took over musical duties. She decided that it would be a good idea to play the 33 RPM records at 45 RPM. The result was that "Abide with me" came out more like "I see a red door, and I want it painted black", as sung by Mick Jagger. The congregation, average age over eighty, was befuddled.

Then there was the Reverend William James Grant. A convivial and sociable man, who liked a gin and tonic, he went on to greater things and ended up the Archdeacon of Tuam in Galway sometime in the 1980s. A highly intelligent man, he was clearly destined to rise in the Church of Ireland, above his position as Rector in Fethard-on-Sea. He may have been fond of a tipple, but that side of his life was all under control. This was certainly not the case with one of his successors.

The man in question, who had better remain nameless, was a hopeless alcoholic. He habitually forgot to put on a dog collar, and showed up for services with a dirty white handkerchief in lieu. This made him look like a rather dishevelled John Wayne in "True Grit". On one occasion he dropped a baby into the font during a christening service. This incensed the parents, who thought the baby too young to go swimming.

His finest hour, so to speak, was to lead the Garda Siochana in a car chase over three counties. He was spotted leaving a pub in South Kilkenny by the Guards and was pursued through Waterford into South Tipperary, when his car ran out of fuel.

One of the Guards in the chasing squad car announced that he now knew what it was like to take part in the 24-hour race at Le Mans. Sadly, a good man brought low by the demon drink.

Recently, my son James got married in Killesk. It was a great occasion. The church was packed, with some outside. I feel sure my parents were looking down on us all with approval. Rather unusually for a Church of Ireland church, Killesk is in excellent condition. The 2nd Lord Templemore would be pleased with the result of his fund-raising.

The Garda Siochana in hot pursuit of the well refreshed Rector. Somewhere in South Kilkenny.

CHAPTER THREE

The Pony Club and learning to ride

It has been a fact of life that for generations rural Ireland has been in thrall to the horse. Racing, particularly National Hunt racing, has long assumed the mantle of a national sport in a way that it never has in England.

In the 60s some of Ireland's most famous names were from the world of racing. One need only mention the names of Tom Dreaper, Pat Taaffe, and Arkle for that to become obvious. These were household names even for people who were not that interested in the sport.

However, we can't all win Cheltenham Gold Cups, and, after the war, what really took off in Ireland was the Pony Club. Lots of lads, and they were mainly lads, aspired to be the next Pat Taaffe, and sure enough some of them managed it. My introduction to the Pony Club and my efforts to learn to ride took place at Mount Juliet, aged about 8, under the tutelage of June McCalmont (more of the McCalmonts later). June founded and ran the Kilkenny Pony Club, and so started for me a lifetime love affair involving the horse.

June McCalmont was generous to a fault, and provided me with my first pony, called Flash. Flash had started out a grey. By the time I got hold of him he was snowy white. He suffered badly from eczema or sweet itch, as it was known. We had to treat the poor pony with some kind of unpleasant looking paste to soothe his sores.

The paste dried on the sores and then started to flake off. The result was that I normally performed in Pony Club competitions looking like some kind of snowman, or even a builder's mate covered in plaster dust from a building site.

Chich and myself took to the pony world like the proverbial ducks to water. It was around this time that Joan Price of Kilmokea, aided and abetted by Boodie Cairns of Alderton House, managed to start a Wexford branch, so we could happily transfer our allegiance from Kilkenny to Wexford. That Club flourishes to this day. It is fair to say that it never looked back, and was responsible for producing a number of competent jockeys of one sort or another. The main problem for my parents was getting their

Boodie Cairns with two of her protegees. This photograph was taken shortly after the great lady had given a lecture to the Wexford Pony Club on the importance of smart turn out of both horse and rider. It must have been gratifying for her to see that her words had been taken to heart by Charlie and Jenny Berridge..

two elder children adequately mounted. My younger sister inherited Flash, so my father had to get his cheque book out. Chich ended up with Rusty, a wonderful 14-2 hands bay mare, and I got Smokey Joe, a tough 13-2 hands Connemara with an attitude problem. Smokey Joe came from a Garda sergeant in Dublin and my father was incensed that he had to pay £100 to get the pony. He implied that not only did the pony have an attitude problem but the Garda sergeant did as well.

Smokey, on his day, was brilliant. When it was not his day, which was most of the time, he could be as uncooperative as only ponies can be. He was a great hunting pony, but not the best in cold blood.

In those days there was an All-Ireland one-day event competition with pony clubs coming down from the north to compete against all the southern clubs. This was needle stuff, and the rivalry was fierce. For a couple of years, the Wexford Club did adequately but no better. Then the great day came when the competition was held in Wexford. We simply had to win.

The Wexford team that day was my sister Chich, myself, Michael Hickey from Garryrichard, on a lovely roan pony called Rosie, and Ted Power, from the Hook, on Billy, a dun pony that was no oil painting, but could perform.

Miraculously we won by the narrowest of margins, a solitary pole down being the difference, beating a strong team from Limerick which included Edward O'Grady, the well-known National Hunt trainer.

The winning team of the All-Ireland competition was always then qualified to compete in the UK championships against the best of the English. I think the rough and ready Irish teams were always viewed with mild amusement by the smart English clubs, but never mind.

Disaster struck me personally when Rusty put her foot through the floor of the horse box, and had to be withdrawn. My replacement was Ted Power's younger brother Con on a coloured pony called Corofin. Con went on to represent Ireland at show jumping as part of the Army Equitation school, and is the father of Robbie Power who rides for Jessica Harrington, and is the winner of Grand Nationals and Gold Cups. I certainly had an able substitute to take my place.

The finals that year, 1968, were held on the racecourse at Cheltenham. The Wexford team did well enough, but were let down by their dressage scores. One thing I remember well, because it infuriated my father, was the English dressage judge, a retired General, writing in his remarks column that Michael Hickey did not understand the Aids (a riding term).

As the Hickey family of Garryrichard had forgotten more about horsemanship than the judge was ever likely to know, this remark did not improve Anglo-Irish relations. My father – who actually knew the judge from his army days – said that he, the judge, was almost stone blind, and therefore couldn't see what was going on anyway.

The next year, the team was slightly different, but we won the All-Ireland again by a rather larger margin. The team was Ted Power, Con Power, a boy called Joe Scallan, and myself on a new horse called Mr. Tod. Mr. Tod jumped for fun but had a pathological loathing of dressage arenas and dressage judges.

The finals in 1969 took place at Stoneleigh in Warwickshire. Just before doing my dressage test there was a shower of rain, and Mr. Tod slipped up while we were practising. The result was that I entered the dressage arena covered in mud, grass stains, and worse. I distinctly remember a very severe looking lady judge, inspecting me disapprovingly over her "pince-nez." I could imagine her comments as follows- "Look at the state of these Irish -

they really are beyond the Pale." My reply, if I had had the chance, would have been, "Well, yes, Ma'am, you are spot-on there. Since Wexford is 100 miles from Dublin, we are beyond the Pale in every sense of the word."

The Wexford team occupied four of the last ten places on the scoreboard after the Dressage element of the competition. While we did four double clear rounds across country and in the show jumping, it was far too big a

Competing on Mr. Tod at the Pony Club championships at Stoneleigh in 1969. Not a dressage judge in sight

deficit to make up. We all thought the Cross Country was far too easy. My father described it as a flat race. So back across the Irish Sea we went, bloodied, or in my case muddied, but unbowed.

Another prominent name competing at the time was Jim Wilson of the Carlow Pony Club. Jim, who has recently died, won the Cheltenham Gold Cup on his mother's horse Little Owl in 1981. Until Sam Waley-Cohen won on Long Run in 2011, Jim was the last amateur jockey to have won it – a distinction he held for 30 years.

My father did a lot of the riding instruction in the Pony Club himself. While he was perfectly competent, he realized that the Achilles heel of all the membership was the Dressage element. To try to raise our lamentable standard, he recruited a number of outsiders to see if the gap with the smart English clubs could be closed in any way. Two of the best he produced were both military men, Colonel Stug Perry, and Corporal Major Jock Ferrie.

Stug Perry, who had been a Colonel in the 9th Lancers, had been brought up, like my father, as a devotee of the Weedon school of riding. Weedon is a village in Northamptonshire which housed the Army school of equitation. (Those were the days). It was here that generations of soldiers were taught to ride. Before the Berlin Olympic Games of 1936, the British equestrian teams were based here, and it was where a lot of the best riders were trained.

The Weedon School taught a distinctive style of riding. Recruits were made to ride with a long leg (referring to the stirrup length), and many hours were spent riding without stirrups and even on occasions without reins. The riding instructors came up with some great expressions, the most famous of which was probably, "Who told you lot to dismount?" when the entire class happened to fall off, which they did all the time.

My memory of Stug Perry was of a man with great charm, rather austere, but with a kindly twinkle. He was probably better known for his skill as a yachtsman. To prove the point, he won an Olympic Silver medal at the Melbourne Games in 1956, and then won the Yachtsman of the Year award. Jock Ferrie was probably a better instructor. He, too, was a devotee of the

Weedon style. He had been a Corporal Major in the Blues, later the Blues and Royals. He was a great man, with the full range of army witticisms. As I was to join the Army two or three years after being chastised by Jock Ferrie, I should have known what was coming.

Both Colonel Perry and Corporal Major Ferrie tried their hardest, but they were really up against it. The attitude of the Wexford lads to dressage, and they were nearly all boys, could be summed up thus: "Let's get this nonsense over as quickly as possible, and get on with the serious business of jumping fences at speed." The result was that movements in the dressage test, that should have been conducted at a collected trot, were quite likely tackled at something more like a loose rein gallop. The severe lady with the pince-nez had a point.

My final recollection of the Pony Club in that part of the world happened later – probably in the 70s. There is a great Kilkenny family called Lambert who lived at a lovely place called Dysertmore high up on the bank overlooking the river Nore. Major Desmond Lambert had been the Adjutant of the Irish Guards Battalion, and by all accounts the smartest officer they had.

The wedding of Major Desmond Lambert to Miss Olive Eustace-Duckett. Of Particular interest is the way Social and Personal described itself in those days. It just goes to show how the meaning of some words has changed!

Desmond and Ollie, his wife, used to host the annual Pony Club hunter trials for the Kilkenny branch. In those days, a lot of the fences had knockable poles, and there was a penalty for knocking a pole down. I forget what the penalty was, but it did exist. As a result, correct scoring was essential, and this was done with score sheets, which were all handed in to the scoring trailer, and totted up to produce a result.

On this particular day, the scorers were under the command of Captain Anthony Tupper, Royal Navy (Retired). As his helpers, he had Paddy Fenlon, an auctioneer from Taghmon in County Wexford, and, I think, Edric Dowley from Kilkenny. The Dowleys were a great horse family from that county.

My father riding at Castletown. The Weedon style, not popular today with the long stirrup length, but effective.

All was going well, and everything was being conducted with military precision, as you can imagine. Then at midday, Paddy Fenlon announced that he had a litre bottle of Bushmills in his car, and that a sharpener might be called for. That is when the wheels fell off in a major way, and the day descended into pure farce.

With the arrival of the Bushmills, the scoring got slower and slower. Voices were raised in the scoring trailer, and it became clear that the Royal Navy's finest was attempting to inculcate his companions in naval terminology. Shouts of "Splice the mainbrace", "Ship ahoy", and "Break out the rum ration", could be heard echoing down the Nore valley – odd really, since Dysertmore must be thirty miles from the open sea.

It was around this time that Anne Tupper, Anthony's wife, arrived with a sumptuous picnic. In a very upper-class English accent, she enquired of the assembled company if anyone had seen, as she put it, "a hungry Tupper." A helpful Irish voice replied "No, Missus, but I can sure hear a thirsty one."

At that moment, out of the trailer, arm in arm, lurched the scoring team, singing a spirited if tuneless rendition of "A life on the ocean wave". Anne Tupper took one look at this motley crew, grabbed her husband by the ear, and, with imprecations of "I'll give you a life on the ocean wave", frog-marched him to her car and then home. It is fair to assume that the Royal Navy's finest was sent to his hammock with no extra rum ration, and probably no ship's biscuit either.

The competition was declared null and void. It had to be, since the score sheets were indecipherable. The red rosette was given to a small boy on a bolshy pony, who had failed to negotiate any fence at all. This was considered a fair result in the circumstances. A lot of the assembled company then descended on the Spotted Dog pub in Inistioge, where more spirited if tuneless renditions of "A life on the ocean wave" could be heard way into the small hours. A good time was had by all.

As a postscript to this fiasco, I should say that my parents were very fond of the Tuppers. They were saddened when they decamped to Cornwall. Anne had come from Cornwall. Her maiden name was Bolitho, and the

Bolithos are a strong Cornish family. Anthony Tupper had inherited a property in Kilkenny from his great-grandmother. The property was called Leyrath. Anthony had built up a prize-winning herd of Jersey cattle, and had put his heart and soul into Kilkenny and Ireland. He made one fatal mistake: he became a member of Lloyds. As a result, Leyrath had to be sold in the early 1990s.

Anthony, as well as many others, including myself, had made the awful error of trusting people who couldn't lie straight in bed if you paid them, which of course we did, many times over. The truest remark I ever heard about Lloyds membership was voiced by another victim who said, "If you can afford to be a member of Lloyds, you don't need to be, and if you need to be a member, you can't afford to be." I forget which member of the Council of Lloyds it was, who was overheard quoting Calvera's dictum in "The Magnificent Seven": "If God did not want them sheared, he would not have made them sheep." This in respect of all the outside names at Lloyds, which says it all really.

I got away from Lloyds, battered and bruised but more or less afloat. Others were not so lucky. I remain convinced that Lloyds of the 1980s and 1990s was one gigantic Ponzi scheme. I am told that the management of Lloyds these days is a model of probity and rectitude – well maybe.

CHAPTER FOUR

Hunting in Wexford and Kilkenny

I was doing a small calculation the other day, and, now that I no longer get on a horse, I was trying to work out how many different packs of hounds I had hunted with in my life.

I ran out of fingers. I think the score was ten in Ireland, and about fifteen in England and Scotland. All of these hunts had fun in their own way. Some were smart, or thought they were, and some had no pretensions at all. I hunted from around my sixth birthday in 1958 till I finally gave up when

Self, my mother, and Chich hunting with the Wexford in the early sixties. I am on Smokey Joe, a great hunting pony but as bolshie as they come when he wanted to be.

my last good horse dropped dead under me in about 2008. If those dates are correct, then I had fifty years of memorable times in the saddle.

In all that time, and with all those packs of hounds, there were none to beat the Kilkenny and the Wexford hounds of the 1960s. People talk about a golden age of this and that, but those packs in that decade produced sport of the very highest order. I was just so lucky to have been present at the time.

My earliest hunting days were with the Wexford hounds. Wexford, or that part of the County hunted by the pack that bears its name (there are other packs in the County) was a country of big banks and ditches. Many of the obstacles were double banks, meaning that there was a ditch on both sides. Particularly on a pony, it was often not possible to jump onto the top of the bank. Therefore, you had to jump onto the face of the bank, and scramble the rest. As the bank was sure to be covered in a proper jungle, the whole obstacle presented a real challenge to horse and rider. It was not for the faint-hearted. There were parts of the country that had dry banks, which had no ditches, but those were the exception.

To begin with, the hounds were hunted by a man called Paddy Pickersgill, who went off to the Galway Blazers about 1960. I was too young to remember much about him or what he did, but, by all accounts, he was a very good huntsman, and showed excellent sport. There was then a bit of an interregnum, till the next full-time master arrived. He was called Julian Spring, and came from Dorset. Julian was a first-class huntsman and took to the formidable Wexford country immediately. He was, however, a rather prickly character, and not easy to deal with as far as money was concerned.

After three or four seasons when the hounds hunted very well, the simmering resentments in the Hunt all seemed to come to a head. It is a sad fact of life that hunting people only seem to be truly happy when they are fighting each other. I have seen that again and again.

The "casus belli" on this occasion was the inevitable money, or lack thereof. The precise issue seems to have been the failure of the committee to make promised repairs to the kennels. I still have in my possession Julian

Spring's letter to my father, who was the chairman of the Hunt. It is a very rude letter, in particular castigating the Hunt secretary, who was a man called John Boyd. The Boyds were an old Wexford family, and John did not deserve such abuse. No doubt there was right on both sides. There always is in hunting rows.

The upshot of all this was that Julian Spring resigned in August, giving the Hunt no time to find a replacement. It is a hunting convention that

Julian Spring with the Wexford hounds in 1963. He was a first rate huntsman, but a prickly character.

"Andy the horse reporter" riding Sandhopper.

mastership arrangements for the following season should be in place by the end of May. Julian Spring had ignored this convention, putting the Hunt in quite a spot.

One light-hearted incident did occur during Julian Spring's mastership, which involved a visit from the hunting correspondent of the Field magazine. This man had the unforgettable name of Sir Andrew Horsbrugh-Porter, the 3rd baronet no less, and one well aware of his social position. Riding one of my father's hunters he came out at a meet of the hounds. As his photograph would suggest, he was a decidedly pukka sort of chap. At the meet he was introduced to a local farmer, who was very deaf, and the pair of them chatted away quite amicably. Things took a turn for the worse when John Boyd joined them and Sir Andrew was introduced as "Andy, the horse reporter from some magazine". Sir Andrew was furious, most likely because that was what he was.

To fill the gap, my father became a joint-master with Victor McCalmont from Mount Juliet, and Robert Moreton who for a short time was married to Victor's daughter Diana. Victor came down from Kilkenny twice a week to hunt the Wexford country, while continuing to hunt the Kilkenny hounds on maybe three days a week. My mother always maintained that the strain of hunting two packs of hounds at the same time probably shortened Victor's life. He certainly rescued the Wexford hounds, and got precious little thanks for it in some quarters.

All this time the Wexford hounds had a loyal Kennel Huntsman in the shape of Ted Fitzsimmons. Ted had started his life with the Kildare hounds, and his proud boast was that in the hunting season he only got to see the kennels, where he lived, in daylight on Sundays. They hunted six days a week, hacked to all meets, so left the kennels in the dark and returned in the dark. You could always tell when Ted was coming up behind you on his horse. All you could hear was the clink-clink of the bottles of Baby Powers in his pocket. No-one ever knew how much Irish whiskey he got through in a day, but judging by the rattle of the bottles it was a fair bit.

After the rescue operation headed by Victor McCalmont came a delightful man called Colonel Neville Cairns. He was not a great huntsman, being rather slow, nor was he a great rider, but he was a charming man whom everybody liked, and, after the preceding ructions, that mattered more than anything. He fell off his horse stone dead, sometime in the early seventies. People at the time remarked that it was the ideal way to go.

Neville was married to one of the great characters of the time. As mentioned in an earlier chapter she was known as Boodie. Boodie was a wealthy woman, the daughter of Sir Dymoke White of Whites the chemist. She always wore the same footwear, which

Major Victor McCalmont – One of the finest huntsmen of his generation and surely the most generous.

consisted of gym shoes and ankle socks. She was perfectly happy wearing these in a blizzard in January. As far as smart dresses were concerned, these were not for Boodie, on the grounds that there was, in her words "a very substantial acreage involved". She devoted a lot of her fortune to providing ponies for local farmers' children. She would haul some unsuspecting ten-year-old out of a farm in the back of beyond, and take them around the country competing in shows, and other competitions. She was incredibly well read, and could complete the Times crossword puzzle in no time at all. All sorts of diplomats have struggled to improve Anglo-Irish relations with limited success. If they had wanted a lesson in how to do it, they should have looked no further than Boodie Cairns.

Her diplomacy did let her down on the odd occasion. One day she encountered Mocken Roche, the mother of Julie Berridge, who was a member of the Pony Club, and therefore a protegee of Boodie's. This meeting, which was fairly one-sided, took place in South Street New Ross – a busy street in a fair-sized town.

Now Boodie had a voice that would put a Guards Sergeant Major to shame, so all the shoppers got the benefit of this gem. "Mocken, I am a bit worried about Julie going off to this quiz competition in Cork. There are two boys with her". She then named them both. "The first is a kleptomaniac, and the second one stinks. I hope she will be

"Anyone seen the fox?" Gordon Doyle, Michael Hickey (senior), and Ollie Lambert. Many people rated Michael Hickey one of the best horsemen in Ireland. There cannot have been many better. He rode many winners at the RDS.

Major Victor McCalmont with the Kilkenny Hounds.

alright". If the good citizens of New Ross did not know of the foibles of these two lads before Boodie's intervention, they certainly did afterwards. Mocken beat a hasty retreat to the butchers.

When I got a bit older, my parents used to drive us all up to the best of the Kilkenny meets. The Kilkenny hounds then, and now, were kennelled at Mount Juliet, the magnificent McCalmont estate.

On my first day out, I was confronted with a sight that I will never forget. I saw the old Major, Dermot McCalmont, who seemed an impossibly old man, mounted on an equally old (or so it seemed to me) grey horse. In fact, it was snowy white, probably due to age. Riding along with him were two liveried second horsemen to see that he was OK, and no doubt to open gates for the old chap. The Mount Juliet hunt staff wore immaculate grey livery, and this was the smartest thing I have ever seen in the horse world. The two second horsemen in grey and the Major in perfect red coat, and champagne-topped boots that shone so much you could have shaved in the reflection, presented an awe-inspiring sight for a small boy. This was hunting in a style that you never see today.

The Kilkenny was effectively a private pack, and the family had two notable hunt servants. The first was Alf Wright from Yorkshire, and the second Paddy Macdonald, a local man. They were expertly schooled in their duties, and added hugely to the quality of the sport with their professionalism. The whole thing ran like clockwork. It was small wonder that there was a queue a mile long to witness this performance.

Some of the most famous meets were a byword in hunting circles at the time, the pick of the bunch being, probably, those meets that were strung along the main Waterford to Dublin road. Names such as Mullinavat East, Mullinavat West, Lukeswell, and Ballyhale spring to mind. Other fine meets were held at Windgap, Kilmaganay, and Boolyglass.

On one occasion at Ballyhale, which was primarily a stone wall country, PP Hogan, the legendary horse dealer from Limerick, got in on the act. Major Victor had momentarily lost touch with his hounds who were away on a fox, but where? PP, who ended his life almost stone blind, claimed at the time to have the very best of hearing. "I hear them, Major, I hear them. They are this way." He then proceeded to lead the field including the Major at breakneck speed over all the best and biggest of the Ballyhale country. It was the hunt of the season, or any season for that matter. There was only one problem – PP had made it all up. The hounds had gone 10 miles in the opposite direction, and he had never heard them at all. The Major was not amused, but we were.

Major Victor's wife Bunny, was a larger-than-life figure, who was well known for her repartee, and general witticisms.

At one stage in the 1970s, Sir Max Hastings took advantage of Ireland's favourable tax laws for writers and poets, and arrived to stay for a few years

How times change. An unknown lady with two Wexford farmers, Jer O'Leary and Walter Kent. Rat catcher with flat cap was normal attire. Today, the poor men would probably be sent home by the health and safety police.

very close to Mount Juliet. Presumably the future editor of the Daily Telegraph qualified as a writer, since I never heard that he wrote poetry.

To amuse himself, he took to the hunting field, which by all accounts was not an unqualified success. Eventually he decided to tackle the formidable Kilkenny country on foot, convinced that he could keep up with arguably the finest pack of hounds in Ireland. He was wrong.

After a particularly gruelling hunt our hero was to be seen staggering along, several fields behind the action with his trousers ripped to the crotch, to the extent that he was hardly decent. Bunny was asked by one incredulous lady, who that astonishing figure was with rather too much on display for polite society. In her own inimitable way, Bunny offered this by

Peter McCalmont chatting up the ladies (after a fashion). The lucky ladies are Pat Trench from Galway, and Heather O'Neill Flanagan from Waterford. Bunny McCalmont in the background has said something hilarious.

way of explanation. "I suppose he thinks it pays to advertise." Yes, indeed!

Mullinavat West was probably the best meet of them all, and sometime in the 1960s CJ Haughey (Charlie) attended this great occasion. He was then an aspiring politician, but later the Taoiseach of Ireland. We were all out as a family that day, and a great day it was too. When the Major blew for home about 4 o'clock, the whole field descended on the VAT pub in Mullinavat. The VAT was a large establishment and it needed to be. My father wrestled his way to the bar in order to get my mother and his three children a drink. Reaching into his pocket, he came out with a fiver.

"Put that away, Lord," says the barman, "Mr. Haughey is buying drinks all round." "Jolly good," said my father. With an instruction to the barman to make his a large one, he trousered the fiver. At about that time word got around the village that Charlie was buying and there was a mad rush for the VAT pub, by assorted local drunks. What the future Taoiseach's bar bill was, was never revealed, but it must have been huge.

Three Majors – George Murray-Smith, my father, Desmond Lambert – Hunting in Kilkenny

The VAT was a great pub, and a favourite of the hunt followers. Things did not always go according to plan though. One day two young blades came down from Dublin, and had a great day, such a great day, that they drank themselves senseless in the VAT afterwards. They ended up, one passed out on top of the billiard table, the other passed out underneath. That was where they spent the night.

Their unforgivable sin was to forget their horses. Those poor animals spent the night in the trailer with all their tack on and not even a bucket of water. Those that knew him well said that the Major was more upset and angered by this episode than almost any other. The two culprits were banned for life, and quite rightly. The two Majors, Dermot the father, and Victor the son, were the most enthusiastic fox hunters ever, but they were both humane men and generous to a fault. Leaving your horses untended in a trailer overnight was a crime on a par with murder in their eyes.

Hunting pubs have a relaxed view of licensing laws in Ireland, as the following demonstrates. The Kildare foxhounds always met on New Year's Day outside the pub in Dunlavin. One year Pat, Diana, and Bunny Conolly-Carew arrived for the meet a little bit early – 10.45 for the 11.30 meet. They decided to go to the pub for a drink. The pub was open but only the barman was there. Pat ordered three cherry brandies. The response was in the negative. The pub does not open till 11.00 said the barman. "Fine "said Pat, "we will unload the horses, and come back for the drink." "You will do no such thing" replies the barman, "you will have a drink with me while we wait for the pub to open." Rather a fine distinction I would have thought.

One incident comes to mind, at the famous Mullinavat meet. Sometime in the 1960s, a rather smart English gent came down for a day hunting. His trailer had a puncture, so he was half an hour late for the meet.

He leaped on his horse, and set off in the direction he imagined the hunt had gone. After half a mile, with no sign of any hounds, he came across a rustic-looking local, leaning on a gate. Both gate and rustic were getting on in years. The conversation went as follows: "Tell me, my good man, how long ago did the gentry leave?" Rustic reply, "Begob, that'll be about 50 year ago." The rustic was entirely correct, if you know anything of the history of Ireland.

One figure that I can barely remember, but who definitely rates a mention, was Mrs. Olive Hall of Kellistown House in Carlow.

She was a remarkable woman who had the unique distinction of having been Master of the Carlow Foxhounds for forty-five years. Among her many achievements was her role in teaching the reigning monarch, Queen Elizabeth, to ride side saddle. At her funeral two of the eighty-eight wreaths came from the Queen and her mother, Queen Elizabeth the Queen Mother. Such was the esteem in which she was held.

Her daughter, Pug, married my old friend John (Black Jack) Alexander's father, and the great lady passed on many of her attributes to the next generation. She was well known for not suffering fools gladly if at all.

On one occasion, after a particularly arduous day with the Carlow hounds, she returned to her stable to be greeted by the stable lad who

Michael Hickey chatting to Desmond Lambert. At a guess the vehicle would have had little chance of passing its MOT then or ever.

observed the following. "I think the horse is sweating excessively Mam," to which she replied, "Don't be ridiculous man. So would you be sweating excessively if you had just spent the last five hours lodged between my thighs." Answer came there none.

I remain convinced that had Mrs. Hall been launched on a one woman search and destroy mission in the Pacific after Pearl Harbour, the carnage

of Hiroshima and Nagasaki need never have happened. All Hirohito's troops would have long since surrendered to Carlow's answer to Boadicea.

One equally formidable huntress of the time was Lady Molly Cusack-Smith, a famous master of the Bermingham and North Galway hounds. Molly was as Irish as they come, but being a girl with an eye for the main chance, had managed to ensnare a decaying Baronet in his dotage, hence her grand sounding title. The poor man never knew what hit him, and did not survive for long.

Lady Molly had an unconventional approach to the art of venery, which might raise a few eyebrows today. Her hounds always met at some pub or other, and on one occasion she arrived at the pub demanding from the barman "a large brown one". The barman passed her the drink and enquired about the prospects for sport that day. "The prospects are excellent" said Lady Molly, "I have outside in my lorry, a pack of hounds, four horses, and a live fox. Sure, what else do we need?" I am not certain if the Masters of foxhounds Association would approve, but times were different then. The barman went outside to inspect the lorry and reported that the noise from inside the vehicle was enough to "waken the dead".

Mrs. Hall looking as if she is about to devour some unsuspecting stable lad.

With all this fun and both Kilkenny and Wexford showing the best of sport, my parents made sure that they had the best of horses. They had a number of big quality horses. I remember Jumbo, Quicksands, The Clown, and Sandhopper. All their horses, without exception, were bought from the Quigley brothers of Fahree. Pat and Dan Quigley patronized two stallions in particular. Those were Sandyman and Battleburn. Hunting in such

Photo opposite: Chich, my younger sister Julie, self, and my father at a meet of the Wexford hounds at Kiltra house. Kiltra was the home of John Boyd, the long suffering secretary of the hunt.

formidable country, it was vital to have a bold brave horse that jumped. It was not for the faint-hearted of either horse or rider.

What my parents did for themselves, they also did for their children. We had the best of ponies that would jump anything. I shall always be grateful for that.

CHAPTER FIVE
Mount Juliet

No commentary on the South East of Ireland would be complete without a full mention of Mount Juliet. It was and still is the most beautiful estate in Ireland. Perched up on the banks of the River Nore, just a few miles from Kilkenny city, the house was built, and the estate laid out, by the Earls of Carrick. The Earl of Carrick of the day named the estate after his wife, who was called Juliet.

It was not till the McCalmont family arrived that Mount Juliet came into its own. The McCalmont family first of all leased the estate in 1902, and then Sir Hugh McCalmont bought the whole property in 1912. This opportunity arose when the Earl of Carrick lost all his money in the stock market crash of that time.

The Butlers may have been short of cash, Butler being the family name of the Earls of Carrick; the McCalmonts, on the other hand, most certainly were not. Successive generations of McCalmonts have lavished loving care and a considerable fortune on the place, turning it into one of the finest examples of its kind in the land.

It was a tragedy for the family, and for all those friends who had enjoyed the family's hospitality, when it had to be sold in 1987. The origin of the family's financial problems came when a finance minister of the state, one Richie Ryan of the Fine Gael party, changed the tax rules on importing money from abroad. Before his intervention McCalmont money came into the country, largely from Canada, tax free.

Major Dermot McCalmont with his second wife June, on either side of Mrs. Geoffery Brooke. The Major was responsible for Mount Juliet and all its wonders.

Bunny McCalmont with her sons Peter and Harry, at the time of her daughter Diana's wedding to Robert Moreton.

Overnight this capital was taxed as income, at the top rate needless to say – result disaster. If only politicians would leave well alone, everyone would be better off.

Mr. Ryan was parodied at the time as "Richie Ruin" and was responsible for introducing a wealth tax in 1976, which also did grave damage to the McCalmonts, and people like my father who were not in the wealth league of that family, but were still caught because they owned valuable land. The wealth tax was levied on land as an asset, which, in my view, is the most iniquitous of all taxes. It looks at the value of the land with scant regard to the ability of such land to generate an income.

Mount Juliet in the 60s and 70s was Mount Juliet in its heyday. There was nothing to rival it in Ireland. There were two studs – Ballylinch and Norelands. There was over a mile of double bank salmon fishing on the River Nore, which was probably the best beat on the river. There was a cricket ground hosting regular matches, with a pitch of variable bounce. The ball either took your head off, or undid your shoe laces. To cap it all, there was a hunter yard and kennels. The yard had stables for around thirty hunters, and they were all full.

The first I remember of "Big J", as it was affectionately known, was in the time of Major Dermot McCalmont. Dermot married

The Nore in summer from the big house

twice – first to Lady Helen Conyngham, with whom he had a son Major Victor, who succeeded him at Mount Juliet. Second, after Lady Helen died young, he married June Nickalls, and they had three sons – Hugh, Pat, and Mikey.

Major Victor married Bunny Sutton, a marvellous hostess, and they had three children – Peter, Diana, and Harry. These were the people who featured so largely in my youth. Partly because of their great wealth they did everything in a style and at a level that was totally unique in Ireland at that time. I have been to a lot of family estates throughout the British Isles, but I have never seen anything to rival Mount Juliet of those days.

I learnt to fish on the Nore at Mount Juliet. My first expedition was in 1965, when I went with my father, fishing a fly, and myself with a Devon minnow. Major Dermot employed a wonderful character as a ghillie, a man called Paddy Bolger. Paddy was a fund of fishing knowledge, and gloriously idle. Paddy had clearly been given instructions by the Major that I was to catch a fish. He put me in the best spot, in the best pool, called Norelands, where I fished away for 5 minutes before hooking a fish. After a minute my reel fell off, so that was that. I was nearly in tears.

After some time scouring the bottom, the reel was located, and put back

The Nore in flood (later in the year). The house was built by Major Victor for his declining years. The water in front of the house is the great Norelands pool.

on the rod. I will never forget what followed: "Reel in" says Paddy. "I can't" I reply. "It's stuck in the bottom." At which point "the bottom" started to move smartly upstream. As salmon fishermen will know, if you take the pressure off the fish, sometimes they will just go back to their lie, and sit there as if nothing had happened. This is what that fish decided to do. Ten minutes later I had my first salmon on the bank. It was 11 pounds and straight out of the sea.

The fishing was superb. On one memorable morning I caught six fish, all in Norelands, without moving more than 20 yards. We were asked to lunch with the Major, and so, much to my annoyance, we had to leave the river at half past twelve to go up to the big house. On arrival at the house, we were greeted by the Major who looked in the boot and all he said was "not too bad, not too bad. Just remember it isn't always this easy." How right he was, but having just convinced myself that I was the greatest fisherman of all time, I felt about one foot tall. It is remarkable to think of today, but Major Dermot subscribed to the theory that you should not let fishing for money. His fishing was for his friends, and it was never let on a commercial basis. The inevitable result was that it was totally underfished – probably the reason it was so good when it was fished.

I had a fascinating fishing experience at Mount Juliet, which just goes to show that anything can happen in the fishing world. Paddy Bolger, with an unexpected burst of energy, announced that we would fish George's Wall from the far bank, which involved a bit of a trek via the cricket pitch. George's Wall was a funny pool, and normally fished from the house side. The other side was made up of a long wall, hence the name, built probably early in the 19th century. You could not wade. It was simply not possible, and far too dangerous. As it was covered by overgrown trees, you could not really fish from the top of the wall either. There was just one spot at the top of the wall, where you could kneel down, and just flick a lure out about ten yards.

"He is either there or he isn't" says Paddy, and no-one could argue with that. I flicked the Devon out from a position on the wall where I was about eight feet above the pool, and could see right into it. Around came the Devon, and hung for a moment in the current. The next thing I saw was a great white mouth opening and shutting. The Devon disappeared from view, and all hell broke loose.

I was in a terrible position to play a fish, and probably a big one at that. I actually conducted proceedings sitting on the wall, because I could not stand up. With the rod tip pointing down the river, rather than up in the air at sixty degrees, which the experts tell you to do. I could not move because of the overhanging trees.

Had the fish really decided to take off, I would have had no chance. As it was, my luck was in and he stayed in the pool. We got him in somehow. He weighed fourteen pounds and was bang fresh. This was a bit of a triumph, because the odds were not in my favour. I had never played a fish from a sort of prone position before, and I am sure I never will again.

Paddy Bolger, when he was not fishing, had the responsibility of maintaining the cricket pitch which was right opposite the Norelands pool. When there was a match on, and I played in a lot of boys' matches, Paddy was one of the umpires. I doubt if there has ever been a more biased umpire. Mount Juliet got all the borderline decisions, and several that were not even borderline. In one match our best batsman snicked the ball to the slips accompanied by a noise like the crack of a whip.

"Howzat?" says the bowler. "Not out" says Paddy. "Why not?" says the bowler scratching his head. "He never hit it" says Paddy. Dicky Bird would have been proud.

Paddy's obsession in the sixties was the great West Indian side of that time, led by Garfield Sobers. For some reason Paddy kept going on about three players who were arguably lesser lights of that side: Seymour Nurse, Conrad Hunte, and Basil Butcher. They were great players but probably not as good as Sobers, or Rohan Kanhai. I quizzed Paddy about his fascination with those three, and it turned out that on television and in the papers the three named cricketers all seemed to be different shades of black! "That Nurse, he's quite black, that Hunte he's a bit blacker, but as for Butcher he's

The Kilkenny Hounds in full cry. The painting is by Peter Biegl, and is in the possession of Harry McCalmont. The two foremost riders are his parents, Victor and Bunny. The country is the stonewall part of Ballyhale, scene of PP Hogan's hunt that wasn't.

as black as my coal scuttle." Paddy had never seen a black man in the flesh, so the fact that skin pigmentation varied quite a lot was a source of great fascination to him. I once asked Paddy if he would like to have faced Wes Hall and Charlie Griffiths on the Mount Juliet pitch. He replied that he would rather run all the way to Dublin. That would be something for a man who would hardly walk to Norelands from his house, all of two hundred yards!

For some odd reason I fancied myself as a bit of an off-break bowler, until it became clear I was hopeless. The truth dawned on me one day, when I came on to bowl against a man called John Cripps, who had been in the Eton eleven in the 1930s. I think he may have been the Captain. He was a marvellous bat to watch. In order to give the boys a chance he used to bat one-handed, and left-handed, as he was a right-hand bat. I came in to bowl to John Cripps, and he hit me through the covers for four, three balls in succession. The penny dropped. I gave up bowling there and then.

John Cripps had a sad end. He was spraying for greenfly in his greenhouse, and left the door shut, and did not wear a mask. He died a couple of days later from respiratory failure. We were all very sad. He was a very nice man, and a wonderful cricketer. Let it be a warning.

A visiting player hit a ball straight into the Norelands pool, right into the best salmon lie. I would love to say that it hit a salmon on the head and it floated to the top, but poetic licence doesn't stretch that far. It was quite a shot, though, all of seventy yards, and still going up as it reached the river bank.

There were two other notable characters that I can think of at Mount Juliet. The first was Albert the butler. He was the head butler (there were three) for Major Dermot. To put it politely, Albert was a lugubrious character, who did not tell many jokes. At one dinner with my father and myself present, the wine was flowing and everyone was in a very convivial mood. Clearly Albert did not approve. As far as he was concerned all dinners should be conducted in silence.

When the port appeared, Albert carried the decanter around and gave everyone a glass. My father by this time was on top form and was well lubricated. He wasn't alone. The decanter came around for the second time, and when Albert reached my father, the following conversation took place.

"Port M'lord?" "Oh yes please, Albert, that would be most agreeable. Rather." "No M'lord", and with that Albert proceeds on his not-so-merry way. He had clearly decided that my father had had enough and that was his way of saying so. It would be quite wrong to suggest that the Major's parties were drunken affairs. The man himself was really very abstemious. Albert was clearly a paid-up member of the local temperance society. My father was distinctly downcast, and thirsty.

Then there was Fred Hansford, the Major's chauffeur. He was a lovely man, and one of life's gentlemen. When you were bidden for dinner at Big J, you were expected to stay the night. After your car was unloaded by platoons of household staff, Fred Hansford would get in on the act. He would remove the guest's motor car. This was, more often than not, a near wreck. The car would be put under Fred's control. It was cleaned inside and out till it shone, and, remarkably, a full tank of petrol was put in it. It is sad to say that some people developed a habit of arriving to stay with their car running on fumes. Really rather predictable that such generosity should be repaid in this way.

After the estate was sold in 1987, the new owners tried to develop a proper covert shoot. Because of the connection with a famous Japanese car maker, there were often plenty of guns who came from the Orient, many of whom had done little or no shooting. At that time there was a vet in the area called Brian Coad, who used to pick up with an army of spaniels. Brian was rather a friend of mine, and he told me this story.

On one particular shooting day, there was a collection of rather gung-ho shooters, all from the Land of the Rising Sun. Brian thought this could be dangerous, so positioned himself behind a large oak tree on the first drive. The ground was very uneven, so he had to put his arm around the tree for support. He told me afterwards that "the blighters only had my hand to aim at, and I still got shot." Brian was a grand man, who was tragically killed in a car accident involving a boat!

It is only fitting that the last word on Mount Juliet should go to the horse. After all, the McCalmont family and horses of all types were inseparable. As I have mentioned there were two studs called Ballylinch and Norelands. I never did know the difference between the two, or what their respective roles were in the big scheme of things.

In Major Dermot's day, the main stud was Ballylinch, but the Major was best known for being the owner of one of the best two-year-olds ever to race. That horse was the Tetrarch, and he won all his seven races as a juvenile. Red-hot favourite for the 1914 Derby, he was injured at home and never raced again.

The Tetrarch's contribution to the Major's racing operation was far from over, however. The horse founded a dynasty at Ballylinch which was famed for its speed. The horse's most famous progeny was Tetratema, which won the 2000 Guineas in 1920, and several other group races. In Major Victor's day there were no Tetrarchs to be seen. That is horse racing for you, and a horse like the Tetrarch comes around once in a blue moon. Major Victor had at one stage the stallions Sassafras and Jazzeiro. Neither horse achieved much as a sire, despite wonderful pedigrees and successful careers on the racecourse.

The Tetrarch by Nina Colmore (1927). Dermot McCalmont's great racehorse.

When horses get in the blood, they stay in the blood. To this day Harry McCalmont owns and runs the Norelands stud, up above where I had my salmon fishing exploits. Harry has achieved great success in the breeding game, which is something that eluded his father. In 2019 he brought off a remarkable double at Tattersalls. To start with he sold a yearling by Siyouni for 1,300,000 guineas, which for a short while was the top price in the session. This half-brother to 2000 guineas winner Magna Grecia did not sit on top of the pile for long though. An hour or so later, he sold a Frankel colt, a half-brother to Derby winner Golden Horn, for 3,100,000 guineas. These are figures that most breeders can only dream of.

Mount Juliet may no longer be McCalmont property but their influence lives on.

One of the four large houses that I used to frequent, this more than the others, since it is Dunbrody Park where I grew up.

A magnificent sight. Curraghmore from the garden side.

Mount Juliet in its McCalmont heyday. The river Nore flows between the brood mares and the bank under the house.

Another of the four great houses I frequented from time to time This is Castletown in Co.Kildare, the seat of Lord Carew. Michael Hickey (junior), my sister, and self. All ready for the off in the Kildare Hunter trial.

CHAPTER SIX

Costello and other fishing stories

If you were an enthusiastic fisherman in Ireland in the 50s and 60s, one of the great pleasures was to head west to one of the white trout fisheries of Connemara, white trout being the commonly used name for a seatrout. I certainly fell into this category, and looked forward to arriving in Galway from one year to the next.

One of the finest of these fisheries was Costello, some 20 miles from Galway city, which was really two fisheries. When I first went there, the Costello end was under different ownership from the Fermoyle end, despite the fact that both fisheries formed part of the same river system. Rising in the hills to the west of Oughterard on Lough Corrib, the Cashla river connected the Fermoyle end to the Costello end. The system consisted of a mass of lakes, which the river flowed through, all full of seatrout and a few salmon from June to September.

I cannot remember the exact number of lakes, and I certainly did not fish them all, but I think there may have been about twenty. I distinctly remember fishing a tiny lake in the middle of nowhere, and catching a 2 lb. trout. It was called Bonramush, and, according to the ghillie, had not been fished for five years. Most of the lakes had boats on them, but not all. The boat on Bonramush was definitely not seaworthy. We were lucky not to have drowned.

Costello had an interesting history, entirely due to the notoriety of one of its early owners. That man was Joseph Bruce Ismay. He was head of the White Star line, which was the company that owned the Titanic. Born in 1862, and educated at Harrow, which happened to be my "alma mater", he was largely blamed for the disaster that was the sinking of the ship in 1912. Certainly, the inquiry that was conducted by Lord Mersey left no doubt about his culpability.

First of all, he supposedly encouraged Captain Smith to go too fast, at a time of year when icebergs were known to drift south into the path of the ship. Secondly, he cut the number of lifeboats that regulations stipulated, to provide more promenade space. Some of the boats that were available were barely serviceable. To compound all this, he ruined his reputation for ever, by leaving the sinking ship in the last lifeboat to get away. A slogan at the time ran as follows:-

"Women, children, and Mr. Ismay first."

There was public outrage at Bruce Ismay's escape when so many were not so lucky, and he became a social pariah, not welcome in anything like polite society. Consequently, he became a recluse, and retired to Costello Lodge, bought the fishery, and by all accounts became a popular if rather withdrawn owner. Some of the ghillies in the 60s whom I remember, notably Pat McDonagh and Michael Donoghue, often talked about Bruce Ismay with affection. They clearly liked him, and he had the reputation of helping to alleviate some of the extreme poverty that existed in Connemara before the 39-45 war.

By the time my father started to go there, Costello had been bought by a rich consortium, including Major Victor McCalmont, the Earl of Harrington, one or two Americans, and a businessman from Northern Ireland called Pat Herdman.

There were a number of very unruly and entertaining parties which descended on Costello Lodge in the summer holidays of the 1960s. One such party was in full swing when Pat Herdman arrived in a magnificent Rolls Royce. Two likely lads took one look at this motor, and decided that sabotage was in order. They were my cousin Dermot Chichester, and an Irish friend from Harrow, Simon Conyngham.

They thought it would be an excellent idea to put a kipper on top of the Rolls Royce's radiator. Pat Herdman headed for home, and could not understand where the noxious smell was coming from, which grew worse by the day. By the time he discovered the awful truth, it was too late. The Rolls Royce was impregnated with the smell of overheated kipper. Pat Herdman never did discover the identity of the culprits, and the Rolls Royce never did recover its smell of old leather. He was known to the perpetrators as "The hurdy turdy man", after a song out at the time, sung by Donovan, called "The hurdy gurdy man".

Simon was the second son of Mount and Eileen Mount Charles. When their marriage foundered in the late sixties, Simon was invited along to Costello by a wonderful lady, called Liz Burke, who was one of the funniest and cleverest people I have ever met. Mrs. Burke had a butler called Willie Cassidy, inevitably known as Hop Along, and he always came too. He and Simon used to head off to two pubs out on the Carraroe peninsula. The pubs had a great system. At closing time, the Garda squad car would drive out from Galway, to see that the rules were being observed. When the car was spotted, the first pub, which already had its lights darkened, would phone the second pub, half a mile along the single-track road. The second pub would immediately switch off all its lights, and the squad car would head back to Galway, happy that Carraroe had the most law-abiding drinkers in the land.

There was a cook employed on these riotous trips. She was called Ruda

My chidren – James and Katie – with June Campbell, a friend from Scotland, making a takeover bid for Prince Michael's throne on the Saltee Islands. He probably didn't mind.

Rotherham, and did not endear herself to Simon and his chums. Simon, being ever resourceful, managed to locate a spot on the river where there was an abundance of river eels. He had been taught a trick at Slane Castle where he lived, where, if you lifted a stone very slowly, the eel underneath could be grabbed at the back of the head, and chucked onto the bank. He got three of these eels, and transferred them smartly to Ruda's bath. When bathing time arrived, there was a full house in the next-door lavatory, waiting expectantly for what followed. There was a blood-curdling shriek, and a naked Ruda left the bathroom at high speed for the safety of her bedroom. Ever after known as "Ruda the Nuda", her fury was wonderful to behold.

One great character who used to go to Costello was Jock "Snipey" Wilson. Jock was the father of Jim Wilson, mentioned in an earlier chapter. He was one of those people whom it was always fun to have around. However, it would be fair to say that Jock Wilson's vocabulary was fairly limited, and mainly consisted of four-letter words. There was a lovely family who ghillied on Glenicmurrin, the largest and most prolific of all the lakes, whose surname was Costello, which sounds unlikely but was true. None of them spoke any English, only Gaelic, so Jock decided that one week he would make it his mission to teach Matt Costello to speak some English. This project met with only limited success.

At the end of the week, an independent judge was summoned to see how the tuition had gone. Matt had only mastered two words in English. The first was "Row", and the second was "Flip." The actual word used was not "Flip", but another four-letter word beginning with the letter "F". Matt was a bit confused. He had not discovered, because Jock had not told him, which word came first. Apparently, while assisting a rather snooty couple the following week, he tried out his new linguistic skills, with the words in either order. He first informed his guests that he would "Row Flip" and when that didn't go down too well, that he would "Flip row". The couple were appalled, and complained to the fishery manager about the rudeness of their ghillie. The whole episode was blamed quite correctly on Jock Wilson.

Bathtime – Ruda the Nuda beating a hasty retreat to the safety of her bedroom after an encounter with an eel.

A famous fisherman of the time was a chap called Bill Large, who came from Athy in County Kildare. Bill was a very skilled angler whose speciality was catching salmon on the stretch of river closest to the sea, above and below the road bridge. He was adopted by Victor and Bunny McCalmont, who thought he was marvellous. He came to dinner and regaled us all with stories of how he had landed this salmon on a Hairy Mary, or that salmon on a shrimp fly, or whatever. We swallowed it all. The only person who didn't was the fishery manager, called Tom Hodgson, who smelled a rat. Tom did a bit of work with his binoculars, and noticed that Bill Large never caught any fish within sight of the road bridge. He fished there alright, but never caught any fish. After drawing a blank in the bottom pools, he would disappear from view, and an hour or so later would come back with a fish or two. It was well known that, week in week out, the pools in view of the road bridge caught more fish than those a bit further up, where Bill Large was having his success.

Tom Hodgson was no fool, and he laid a trap. Well before Bill Large arrived on the river, he went up stream and hid in a gorse bush with a powerful camera. An hour or so later Bill Large appeared, and as soon as he was out of sight of the road, promptly changed his kit, and put up that well known fly in some quarters, which most people identify as a worm. Almost immediately Bill Large had a fish on. Tom Hodgson appeared from his gorse bush with the words, "That's a very interesting fly you have up, Bill, and I have it all on camera." Bill Large never fished at Costello again.

Our introduction to fishing as children was to go out to the end of the Hook Peninsula, and fish for mackerel off the rocks, just beyond the tiny fishing village of Slade. Great fun it was too. The real treat, though, was to go on a day trip to the Saltee Islands, getting on a boat from Kilmore Quay. The Saltees are one of the great bird sanctuaries of the British Isles. Just about all the sea birds that inhabit these islands are there, including a gannetry which has grown in size in recent years. The smell and noise when the chicks are hatching is quite overpowering.

The islands lie just off the coast of South Wexford, and they have an unusual ownership history. They were bought in 1943 by one Prince Michael Neale. The name causes great confusion. The man was actually christened Prince. It was his name not his title. However, he played up to it in full, as we can see.

After he bought the islands, he put the following notice in the National Papers.

"I, Prince Michael Neale, Landowner, will assume the title of Prince of the Saltees, at the conclusion of the war. Also, I wish it to be known that no-one will be permitted to enter the Saltee islands without a permit issued by me. Anybody caught interfering with the millions of birds and their eggs which inhabit these islands will be severely dealt with."

The busy harbour at Kilmore Quay. From here it is a short trip to the Saltee Islands.

Such an authoritarian diktat was clearly not based in Irish law, but, while eccentric, Prince Michael was harmless enough. He did own the islands, and there is no law, that I know of, stopping him from declaring himself their prince.

I have visited the islands many times, and have sat on Prince Michael's throne, without his raising much of an objection. He had the throne specially constructed for himself, and for his "coronation." Prince Michael was a rich man, having made a fortune in cattle dip, a liquid pesticide, which enabled him to buy the islands in the first place.

His "coronation" took place in July 1956, when Michael, fully robed, sat on the throne and declared himself to be "Prince Michael the First."

Annoyingly, I have never been able to find out who crowned him. I imagine the Archbishop of Canterbury was busy at the time. One of Ireland's true characters, he died in 1998, and is buried locally, and not on his islands. As far as I know the islands are still the property of the Neale family.

One interesting feature of South Wexford was the presence of at least three Martello towers. These towers were built as small defensive fortifications in Napoleonic times. They were round towers with enough height to provide a platform for a single artillery piece. The typical Martello tower was large enough to house maybe 20 soldiers and enough food and ammunition to withstand a limited siege. There are three such towers on the Hook peninsula that I know of. Two of these are just outside Dunbrody Park. These would have been positioned to provide extra protection for Duncannon Fort, less than half a mile away. The third can be found further out on the peninsula, overlooking Baginbun Bay where the Normans landed in the 1170 invasion of Ireland. It may well be that whoever sited the tower at Baginbun had in mind what happened some six centuries earlier.

The Martello tower at Baginbun

We knew the owner of the tower at Baginbun, and I remember going to beach parties there. I always harboured an ambition to own a Martello tower and pretend I was some Napoleonic soldier. Any more of such delusional thoughts, and I will end up like Prince Michael!

Since this chapter is primarily on fishing, I will return to the topic. A fine river I used to go to, on a few occasions, was the Caragh river on the

Iveragh peninsula in County Kerry. The river rises in the hills of the Macgillycuddy's Reeks. It flows into Caragh lake and from there for a couple of miles or so to the open sea at Castlemaine harbour.

One day, fishing with Johnny Alexander, universally known as Black Jack to all his friends, we were having no success with conventional methods. Black Jack decided that drastic measures were called for. He found a stretch of the river which flowed between two high banks forming a kind of gorge. He stationed me on top of the bank, acting as a lookout for both fish and bailiff, since his chosen method was very off-limits.

There had been some rain, so that the river was rather discoloured, but not filthy. I was about 12 feet above the river, looking straight into the depths. My fishing friend then put up an evil looking prawn that had seen better days, and he floated it down the gorge.

The history of Baginbun. If the 100 defenders really did hold off an army of 3000 from Waterford, this is a feat of arms on a par with the 300 Spartans at Thermopylae. Somehow I doubt it.

The first time he did it, I thought I saw a shape or rather a shadow appear in the murky water, and then nothing. I could not be sure. It could well have been my eyes playing tricks.

"Reel in, and do exactly the same thing again, Johnny," say I. So, he does.

Down floats the prawn slightly slower this time. Up from the depths comes a shadow, then a shape, then the back of a decent salmon. "Hold it right there, Johnny. Do nothing." For what seemed like an age the fish, and it was a decent size, sat motionless in the water, maybe a foot downstream of the prawn. It then appeared to nudge it, and, after what must have been a minute, opened its mouth and swallowed the prawn, and went back to its lie. Ten minutes later a fine 8lb. fish was on the bank. I had seen everything from my vantage point. It rather reminded me of my fish at George's Wall at Mount Juliet. This time I had a far better view of what a salmon can do when it takes a fly or in this case a foul-smelling prawn. Salmon do not always act aggressively. Sometimes the whole process is so leisurely that you barely notice it. This fish took a very long time to make up its mind.

One postscript to the Caragh river fish. As a precaution, I had crawled to my vantage point on my stomach. I am pretty sure that if I had just walked up to the rock standing upright, I would have spooked the fish, and that would have been that.

When I was a boy, I remember my father fishing regularly on the Slaney. He was a guest of a man called Admiral Lang. He seldom came away empty-handed. In those days the Slaney was one of the great rivers of the British Isles. It had one peculiarity, which, as far as I know, made it unique. It was exclusively a spring river. It fished well from mid-February till mid-May. After that no-one bothered with it. I took some friends to fish on the Wood beat by Bunclody in July a few years ago. We caught one very old, very small, rather tired cock fish. Everyone thought I was mad to even try.

Later on, I used to go to Clobemon Hall to try my luck, then the property of a man called David Nugent. I became quite a friend of David. One thing I noticed, which perplexed me, was that one or two of his local friends kept referring to him as "the common man." This made no sense to me, since for all the world he seemed to be a prime example of a rich, Old Etonian toff, of impeccable lineage. It was only when it was pointed out to me that David's surname could, without altering the pronunciation, be spelt as "New Gent" that all became clear!

It has always seemed to me that the salmon rivers of the South East are an underrated national resource. These are big rivers with a huge catchment area, stretching from the middle of Ireland to the Wicklow mountains. That is an enormous area. Recent Irish governments have, I think, got the message that a rod-caught salmon is so much more valuable to the national economy than a netted one. Certainly, there has been a concerted effort to dispose of estuarial and other nets. As I happen to own a netting station in my local estuary, I am a bit ambivalent about this "improvement"!

I am about to start on refurbishing the V net, for that is what it is. It is listed in the records as a sprat fishery. This is complete nonsense. All my life it has been used to catch salmon. Stationed where it is, it can take fish destined for all three rivers, Nore, Suir, and Barrow. Catching salmon is now illegal, but it still goes on. It is possible that when I have replaced the decaying timbers, it might resume its original purpose, and be used as a sprat fishery.

A local friend of mine realised that the net was being used to catch salmon out of season. In other words the fish were being poached. To add insult to injury, he poached the poacher, and raided the net before the tenant appeared on the scene. He was in the process of removing no fewer than 28 salmon, when the tenant showed up. There was then a distinct possibility of a naval battle on the high seas. This did not happen for the very good reason that, as the enemy was being engaged, the bailiffs appeared in a rather more powerful boat than those at the disposal of the combatants. The day was saved for my friend and the tenant by the fact that the bailiffs could not make up their mind whom to chase. This episode occurred many years ago, but is still talked about.

CHAPTER SEVEN

Snipe shooting in the wilderness

In the 50s and 60s Ireland had hardly any formal covert shoots in the way that England has had since Edwardian times, and before. There were good shoots at places like Lisnavagh (Carlow), Curraghmore (Waterford), and Coolattin (Wicklow). Nevertheless, they were the exceptions and the Irish have never developed the method of driving pheasants and partridges, to the same extent as the British.

What the South East of Ireland did have in abundance was the ideal terrain to attract the migratory snipe. There were some woodcock, but not in great numbers, since the South East corner is not really on the main migratory route of that bird. For large numbers of woodcock, you need to go to the west of the country – to counties like Cork, Kerry, and Galway.

Three great snipe shooters. My father, Captain Piers Dennis, and Black Jack, planning a manoeuvre on a bog in Carlow I was present on this occasion, and can confirm that Piers did not shoot a Dairy Cow for a change.

We had three circuits of bogs on which to shoot. On the circuit around Dunbrody Park there were maybe six or seven bogs that would all hold snipe at the right time of year, that being December and January. One of our most prolific bogs was the game sanctuary at Ballykelly. It could only happen in Ireland. The second circuit was at Fortgranite in Wicklow, the family home of Piers and Gabby Dennis. Piers was known as "Baldy", for obvious reasons, and he was a wonderful shot and an even better fisherman. The third circuit was at Milford in Carlow. These bogs were under the watchful eye of Black Jack Alexander, he of the evil-smelling prawn.

These were three of the best circuits around, and it was quite possible to shoot 20 to 30 driven snipe in a day. That figure may not sound much, but driven snipe are notoriously hard to hit. The strike rate could easily be as low as one in six or seven. On that basis the team of six or seven guns could easily have fired off 150 to 200 cartridges. Great sport it was, and all conducted in the wildest imaginable country. All you did was surround the bog, and put one man and a dog into the bog and try to shoot the birds that came out.

There were many amusing incidents which inevitably occurred, and I can't remember them all. Here are a few.

Black Jack's best bog was known as the shaky bog, since if you trod on it, the whole bog would tremble. It was probably highly dangerous but we didn't care. Right by the shaky bog was a dilapidated cottage occupied by an equally dilapidated old crone who was known to be cantankerous at the best of times. For all the world she looked like a witch out of Macbeth.

The old man and the sea – Black Jack on his way to the Skelligs.

One day, we arrived as a party of about six at the shaky bog. While assembling guns, and sorting out dogs, out of the cottage shot the old crone in a fury.

"Whadda you doin? Whadda you doin? I'll have ye know my husband is an animal lover." A great friend of mine from Scotland shot back as quick as you like, "So I see." The crone who understood perfectly well what he meant, was so angry she could speak no more, and threatened the assembled company with eternal damnation. It was certainly a quick retort.

One frequent guest at these shooting expeditions was Henry (later Sir Henry, now Lord) Bellingham. Of Irish extraction, Henry is an old friend of mine, and in those days was an aspiring politician. He later became a distinguished Member of Parliament for North West Norfolk.

Henry has always had an individual approach to life, and could be fairly described as mildly eccentric. For some reason, with an election looming in the UK, he thought it a good idea to practise his canvassing on a few unsuspecting locals. A couple of particularly dishevelled locals were greeted as follows: "Good morning, my good men. I trust I can count on your vote next week," this conversation taking place in County Carlow, some 400 miles from Henry's constituency.

Black Jack on his way back from the Skelligs. A rough crossing as he seems to have aged a bit. During his stay someone invented colour photography!

It all proved too much for the dishevelled pair, one of whom responded as follows: "Don't worry, Sean. It's some English Eejit. They always behave like that when they have been on the sauce." Henry won his seat with a thumping majority, but without any help from County Carlow.

Another time shortly after my father had inherited the title of Marquess of Donegall, we were all shooting a bog next to the main Waterford-Dublin railway line. At the time my father had a most unruly black Labrador called Danny. After a gun had shot a snipe onto or near the line, Danny escaped, and, pursued by my father, disappeared up the line in the general direction of Dublin. This just happened to be the time the mid-day express was due, and it was a very close-run thing whether my father would catch up with Danny before the express caught up with both of them.

He got the dog off the line with a few seconds to spare. Amidst all the shouting, and the hooting of the train, Piers Dennis turned to me, and said with a twinkle, "You nearly got promoted there, Packy." It was a very near miss, and the train could easily have got both man and dog. Piers, from Fortgranite, just outside Baltinglass, was a lovely man and a true friend. He was a proper countryman, and, among other things, was a superb fisherman.

I fished down a pool with him on Black Jack's beat on the Slaney. There was too little water, which was clear as gin, and I could have sworn that the pool I fished had nothing in it.

Piers came behind me with a trout rod and a tiny Blue Charm fly. Halfway down the pool, just behind the one and only rock, a fish took. It led him a merry dance, as you would expect on a trout rod. After a great battle, with the fish more in control than the fisherman, I netted it. It weighed just under twenty pounds, and was sitting in water no more than 18 inches deep. Quite extraordinary.

Fortgranite was a famous house in Ireland for two reasons. It had a wonderful collection of Munnings pictures, which in fact belonged to Gabby, and were her pride and joy. The second reason was that in winter, even in a cold spell, the temperature outside the house was normally higher than the temperature inside. People begged Piers to invest in some dry wood, but all we ever got was a wet log spitting in the grate, and giving out no heat at all. Piers was a great devotee of walking up bogs rather than driving them. This was because he was lightning fast, and speed is of the essence when walking up a bog.

Captain Dennis taking extreme measures to repel intruders at Fortgranite.

While Piers was undeniably an expert shot, this expertise on occasions landed him in hot water. I have already mentioned the Munnings pictures, and it would be fair to say that Piers and Gabby had become a bit paranoid as far as the security was concerned. One evening in winter, Piers heard footsteps on the gravel outside. Fearing the worst, that they were about to become the victims of an armed robbery, he went to the gun room and emerged with a twelve-bore shotgun. He opened the window, and shouted at the top of his voice, "Clear off. I have a gun." With that he fired both barrels into the night in the general direction of the footsteps. "That will do the job dear. We won't be troubled by them again."

At the time Piers was a dairy farmer, so it was with more than a little remorse that at daybreak he found one of his best milking cows dead on the gravel, a victim of an unprovoked attack by someone with a shotgun!!

We always had very entertaining shoots at Dysertmore, the family home of the Lamberts. Major Lambert usually had a few pheasants, but not many. I think he knew them all by name, and did not really want to see his friends shot.

However, when one of these birds did take to the air, it was accompanied by a roar from the Major of "Cock up". A fellow pachyderm from the valley below, normally my very great friend Dennis Critchley-Salmonson, would trumpet a response along the lines of "Known that for years Major, but where are the pheasants?" Dysertmore was a peaceful spot, so it seemed incongruous that on occasions the quiet would be shattered by one hundred decibel shouts of "Cock up", or indeed "Break out the rum ration." An innocent passer-by could be excused for wondering what on earth was going on.

Just south of Carlow town lies the Milford estate. With the house now sold, it had belonged to the Alexander family for generations. The Alexanders were originally a Northern Irish family, and had made their money as millers. In fact, a previous Alexander had built Milford mill, a huge building. My great friend was Black Jack, who features throughout this book. He was a great Irish character, whom everybody misses. A larger-than-life figure, his hospitality was legendary, and the scrapes he got into equally so. He was a talented engineer, and he started two hydro-electric schemes. One was on the Barrow in Carlow, just outside his back door, the other on a river in Kerry close to where he had a house.

For whatever reason, the Kerry scheme was much more successful than the Carlow version. Just when the Kerry scheme was really moving into profit, Black Jack was upended by the gangsters in that well known London insurance market, and he had to sell his gem of a scheme to pay off his Lloyds losses.

Black Jack had an uncle called Ken Alexander, who was a very old man when I knew him. In his later years he went completely mad, but lived in a bed on the ground floor at Milford. Let it never be said that the Irish don't look after their own. One day after snipe shooting, the six or seven snipe shooters were having tea and crumpets, and maybe something a little stronger, in front of a roaring fire. We were suddenly startled to hear a bellow from the general direction of Uncle Ken's bedroom. We listened intently, and heard the following words of command :-

"Hold hard on the left. Forward on the right. Steady the 12th Lancers. Trumpeter sound the charge." Black Jack shook his head, and told us that it went on all the time. According to him Uncle Ken was reliving the battle of Omdurman, or maybe Waterloo. It certainly made for an unusual tea.

Black Jack had a younger brother, Brian, always known as Broosy. The two brothers had what can best be described as a volatile relationship. Just before the occasion of Jack's 50th birthday party at Milford, the brothers' relationship was enduring a low point. The "casus belli" was, allegedly, that Jack had stolen

Broosy Alexander in customary pose. Beer and fag to hand.

Broosy's girlfriend. The girl in question was blissfully unaware that she was romantically entangled with either brother, but never mind, that is a minor detail.

To level the scores, Broosy decided to sabotage the party at Milford, to which all of the great and good of Carlow and the South East had been invited. Broosy himself had been disinvited. His method of sabotage was as follows: he waited till the party was in full swing, and the champagne, whiskey, and assorted cocktails were disappearing at speed. Then he

Broosy Alexander's wedding to Sheila – From the left Johnny O'Brien, Pug Alexander, the bride and groom, Johnny Alexander, and John Skeffington later the 14th Viscount Massereene and Ferrard – Sheila's nephew.

climbed a ladder, and got onto the roof at Milford, found the chimney which serviced the roaring fire in the sitting-room, and sat on the chimney-pot.

The result was instantaneous. The party came to a disastrous conclusion, when the entire house was engulfed in smoke, and the great and good decamped in a hurry to a very cold garden, coughing and spluttering. The assembled company put the match score at 5-0 to the younger brother.

Broosy eventually left Ireland, probably because the country was not quite big enough to accommodate the pair of them. He left Carlow for Kent, which must have been a bit of a culture shock. However, Sheila, his wife, came from there, so it was an understandable move. He never really settled in Kent, which was rather too boringly respectable for his liking. He did, though, find one agreeable watering hole that was prepared to tolerate this eccentric Irishman. The pub was in the local town, possibly Tenterden, a classic home for stockbrokers. At that time Broosy owned a Labrador bitch which he had christened "Sex". I suppose having a dog called "Sex" in a place like Tenterden was always going to lead to trouble, and so it did.

One evening in the pub, while Broosy was getting the better of half a dozen pints of the local brew, Sex got bored and left the pub and went home which was only half a mile away. After a while Broosy followed rather unsteadily. He was weaving his way up the high street, when he happened to bump into two police officers out on patrol. The conversation went as follows :

"Good evening, Sir. Are you alright? You appear to be a little wobbly." Reply- "It's OK, Officer, it's OK. I am just out looking for Sex." The long arm of the law took a very dim view of this pronouncement, and Broosy had to accompany the boys in blue back to the station. Broosy died from leukaemia sometime in the early eighties. With his passing Ireland lost one of its unique characters. Any man with a dog called Sex, and his best hunter called The Yellow Submarine, is a man to be reckoned with.

CHAPTER EIGHT
Other characters

This chapter is devoted to some of the other characters who went to make this part of Ireland such a pleasure to grow up in. To describe them as an interesting and varied bunch does not do them justice.

One of the most notable personalities in this part of Ireland must have been Tyrone Beresford, the 8th Marquess of Waterford, who lived not far from us on the magnificent Curraghmore estate near Portlaw in County Waterford. Tyrone was a friend to many, and an object of fascination to all. He was eccentric for sure, but he lived in grand style, and was a far more accomplished and able man than a lot of people gave him credit for. He ran a top-class shoot, where he did most of his own keepering. I was lucky enough to have half a gun there for several years, and it was all made such fun by Tyrone and Caroline, his wife. While he was a fine shot, his real forte was on the polo field where he was a regular team mate of the Duke of Edinburgh.

On one occasion Tyrone was travelling in the same car as my father, and a charming man called Dayrell Gallwey. I forget the precise circumstances, but it was on some sort of shooting trip. As the party was negotiating the bridge in Waterford City the car happened to be stopped by the Garda Siochana – nothing wrong, just checking. The garda, who was a strict officer with not much sense of humour, took a look inside, and, turning to my father, asked his name.

"Donegall", said my father. "And what might your name be?" Looking at Tyrone, "Waterford" says Tyrone. "And yours?" Looking in the back at Dayrell. "Oh. Gallwey."

The 8th Marquess of Waterford dressed for his favourite activity. He was a skilled polo player but his brother Lord Patrick Beresford was probably better.

The Beresford family outside the main entrance at Curraghmore.

"I see", says the garda, "We have a right bunch of jokers here. For your information, I am the Rock of Cashel. I asked for your names, not where you live. Get out of the car." It took some time to placate the furious garda, and convince him that the three men really were all called the names they said. He went away muttering, still convinced that they were taking the "you know what."

My father had another brush with the long arm of the law involving a shotgun. On his way south from shooting somewhere North of Dublin, he decided it would be a good idea, which it wasn't, to give his dog a run and clean his gun on the side of the Naas dual-carriageway, just south of the city. An alarmed member of the public phoned the Guards, and reported that there was a lunatic brandishing a gun on the side of the road. My father was duly detained, and given a very serious talking to. These days he would probably have been shot dead.

I shot in Wicklow with Tyrone, where he had a grouse moor. This moor was just south of the Poulaphouca reservoir, which supplies Dublin with a lot of its water. We walked up grouse in the morning, and went racing at the Curragh in the afternoon. I am not sure, as a sporting day, that can be bettered. While there were a few grouse, only Tyrone actually managed to hit any. I think he shot a brace. I fired at one and missed it. I am used to that. I did take the opportunity to read his game books, and was surprised to see that before the First World War there were plenty of days where they shot 50 to 60 brace. You can't do that to-day, but the grouse in Ireland is far from extinct. There are one or two places where a serious effort has been put in to increase the grouse population. It can be done, if enough people put in enough money.

Our next-door neighbours at Dunbrody, when I was a boy, were the Price family – Colonel David, his wife Joan, and Athel, Johnny, and Joanna. Johnny was really my friend, since he went to the same prep school on the same day as me. The prep school was in Kent, quite close to Broosy

Curraghmore from the main drive.

Sir David Ainsworth, and Mr. Don O'Neill Flanagan taking a little light refreshment on a shoot at Curraghmore. Probably not Ribena! Sir David was known to all and sundry as "Decent Dave". I am not sure this was an entirely accurate sobriquet.

Alexander's pub. Why the pair of us were packed off to Kent, I never did discover. It may be a long way to Tipperary, but it was just as far from Kent to Wexford.

Johnny was and is a great man for a party, and he was blessed with a wicked sense of humour. He could be guaranteed to see the funny side of anything. When my younger sister Julie got married, I hired a bus to take wedding guests from London to County Wexford. The bus driver was a simple soul, who had never been to Ireland before, and, from the sound of things, seldom out of Surrey. Johnny hitched a lift on the bus, accompanied by an enormous Persian carpet, for some reason. Maybe the bus provided a convenient and cheap way of transporting such a large item. Johnny chatted up the bus driver, and guessed correctly that here was a sure source of entertainment.

He managed to convince the unfortunate man that where he was heading was a haven for "the men of violence", and that they particularly had it in for English bus drivers from Surrey. His chances of survival were, according to Johnny, very slim indeed. The poor man spent the next 24 hours hiding under a seat at the back of his bus, reduced to a gibbering wreck. John Price Esquire thought it a huge joke. Eventually it was pointed out to the terrified man that the "men of violence" just might have bigger fish to fry than a bus driver from Surrey, with no possible connection to the security forces anywhere, let alone in Ireland.

The Price family once organized a Barn Dance at Kilmokea, which got a little out of control. As the name would suggest it took place in the fairly extensive stables. At the time, Johnny had a piebald pony called Socks, which had to vacate his stable for the evening. A chap called Simon, who was a guest at the party, was hell bent on getting to know a particular girl rather better than he did already. In order to get to "know her better" he selected the empty stable previously occupied by Socks. As he was in the process of getting to know her very well indeed, Joan arrived, looked over the stable door, and with a squawk announced the following :- "You can't do that here. This is Socks' box." It is not altogether clear why Socks would have objected to his box being used in such a fashion. The implication was

Mrs. Hall and her daughters and sons-in-law. From the left - John and Pug Alexander, Mrs Hall, and Barbara and Oliver Hardy Eustace-Duckett. What an honour to have a double champion hurdler named after one.

that such behaviour was fine, just as long as it did not take place in the box normally occupied by Socks – all rather strange.

At the same party the band failed for some reason. Maybe they were tired and emotional, or possibly downed tools to have a bit of supper. As luck would have it, a young chap took over the provision of dancing music, claiming he could sing a bit, and could play the accordion or a banjo of sorts. His name was Chris Davidson of Bargy Castle. He later became the pop star Chris de Burgh. No-one realised it then, but a glittering career probably started at the Kilmokea Barn Dance. You have to start somewhere. I did wonder many years later if "Lady in Red" had been inspired by the goings-on in Socks' box. I am afraid it seems rather unlikely.

The village of Arthurstown, just below Dunbrody Park, has always boasted some unusual characters. Possibly the most unusual, when I was a boy, was a chap called Jamesy Revill. Jamesy was not as others, to use the well-known euphemism. He was more or less manageable when he was on his medication, but if, for whatever reason, he forgot to take it, or, more likely, his poor mother forgot to give it to him, he became dangerously violent.

After one such slip-up, he attacked his mother with an axe. Fortunately, he buried the axe in a wall rather than his mother's head. However, this was the final straw for the local doctor, who packed Jamesy off to the popular lunatic asylum in Enniscorthy, which is a town some 35 miles to the north. The asylum itself was a Victorian monstrosity, but was always full to the brim with inmates, suffering from all kinds of mental illness. As it was always full, it was assumed to be popular.

A few years ago, the Asylum notice board at the front gate, which normally held notices of Church services, sports events, and the like, just happened to be completely empty. This was not good enough for one local joker who wrote on the board in felt pen and large capital letters the following three words:-

MAY CONTAIN NUTS.

Ireland has become a more politically correct country in recent years, and our local wag's attempt at humour was not very well received in some quarters. I was told that the reception was quite different in the local pubs.

A well-known author from the South East was John Welcome. This may have been to a large extent because of his partnership with Dick Francis. John Welcome was, of course, a pseudonym. His real name was John Brennan, a solicitor from Wexford. The Brennans, John, Stella and their children, lived just outside Wexford town. I remember going to children's parties at the Brennan house, and no doubt they came to ours.

Over the years John and Stella became firm friends of my parents, and the two men chatted a lot, nearly always on the subject of the horse. Towards the end of his life, my father was incarcerated in a very good nursing home called Cherrygrove, when he could no longer manage things. One day, I paid one of my regular visits to my father, and found John Brennan in my father's room, having what was clearly an animated discussion.

Not wishing to interrupt the two old men, I settled down to listen to the pearls of wisdom. What followed was a classic of its kind. My father was recounting the tale of how the Kilkenny hounds had had a marvellous hunt from Castle Morris near Kilmaganay. At the same time John Brennan was recounting how Her Majesty the Queen's filly Dumfermline had triumphed in the 1977 Oaks. The filly had been ridden by Willy Carson and trained by Dick Hern. John Brennan spent twenty minutes or so extolling the virtues of the Carson/Hern partnership.

Both men were very deaf. At least my father was stone deaf. It was quite clear that neither man had any interest in the story of the other. After the twenty minutes were up, John Brennan departed with the words, "Lovely to see you Dermy, and I am so glad you agree with me about Willy Carson's riding."

My father replied, "Lovely to see you, John. Before you came, I had forgotten about that hunt. It really was the hunt of the season." Two determined old codgers who would not be deflected. They never saw each other again.

The Leighs of Rosegarland were an astonishing family. The father Francis and the son Robin were more or less certifiable. The show was kept on the road by the mother Winifred, who was English, lived till she was a hundred, and was a trooper to beat all troopers.

My mother complained bitterly, that, when the hunt ball was held at

My contribution to the gaiety of the nation. The maze at Dunbrody Abbey with the Abbey in the background, and the castle on the right. The castle is a folly since it was never lived in.

Dunbrody, which it was for many years, she had to dance with Francis, who, while dressed in smart red tail coat and white tie, always wore hob-nailed boots. These boots did untold damage to my mother's ankles, and the rather fine floors in the room set aside for dancing. You could not call it a ballroom. Robin also attended these parties, and it became clear to all that he had taken a bit of a shine to my elder sister. His intentions towards her became obvious, when he always started frothing at the mouth when my sister came on his radar. This she found disconcerting.

Rosegarland was condemned as not fit for human habitation and demolished. There is no house there now. For many years I had to deliver the Poppy tin to Winifred on behalf of the Poppy Appeal Ireland. I finally gave up when access to the house in a vehicle became impossible. In later years you had to navigate your way through something like the Amazon Jungle. As the tin, when I collected it, never held more than a fiver, it did not seem worth the effort.

Talking of hunt balls, while the Wexford hunt ball took place at Dunbrody Park, an altogether grander affair took place at Castletown in Kildare, the seat of Lord Carew. This was the Kildare hunt ball. It was always well attended, and much enjoyed by the members of the hunt, their guests and the local farmers. There was plenty of "bon viveur" had by all.

Lord Carew was a kindly soul, who enjoyed the good things in life. As well as being master of the North Kildare Harriers he was exceedingly kind to the Kildare Hunt. He was happy to host the ball at his magnificent Palladian mansion, but he did have certain reservations. One of these was an aversion to the press, and anyone taking photographs. As far as he was concerned the ball was a private party, and all in attendance were his guests, which of course they were.

On one occasion in the late 1950s, some young whippersnapper, or at any rate a snapper, started taking photographs of the proceedings from behind the numerous pillars. Lord Carew ordered the whippersnapper to stop.

This he did for a bit, but after half an hour or so, out came the camera again. Snap-snap. Click-click. This was all too much for his Lordship, who, with the assistance of some well-oiled support, ordered him from the house and escorted the miscreant to the front door. The name of the miscreant was Antony Armstrong-Jones.

This is, I think, the only recorded instance of a future spouse of royalty being given the "Bum's Rush" by an illustrious Irish peer from the hunt ball that he was hosting. Well played Lord Carew, I say. That should have put some manners on the man. The future Earl of Snowdon beat a hasty retreat to Leixlip Castle, his billet for the night, with his tail between his legs.

It was a tradition in Lord Carew's day at Castletown that a party was given at which the British Ambassador was the principal guest.

In the late 1950s, the British Ambassador was a charming old boy called Sir Alexander Clutterbuck. On one occasion, the abassadorial car broke down and he was quite late for the party. This gave Murphy the Butler ample opportunity to have a go at the sherry trifle, no doubt dispensing with the trifle.

When Sir Alexander and his wife finally appeared, they were announced by Murphy to a room full of distinguished guests as follows:-

"My Lady, His Excellency the British Ambassador and his wife... Sir Clutter and Lady Buck." No one knew where to look.

Finally, there was the Parish Priest of Ramsgrange, one of the local villages. He was the Reverend Canon Butler, a delightful man, who got on particularly well with my mother. He regularly came to tea, and, as soon as he had settled in to the Earl Grey, and scones, he always said the same thing to the assembled company.

"I want to tell you a story," said the Father. "No, Father. Whatever could that be?" chorused the room, knowing full well what was coming. "Do you know, that before the war I saw Hitler in the flesh?"

This was true. It turned out that, as a young priest, he had been on some kind of retreat to the Vatican, probably in 1937. This trip to Rome had coincided with the Fuhrer paying a visit to Mussolini, so he had been in the same area as those two monsters.

The future Lord Snowdon being sent packing from the Kildare Hunt Ball by Murphy the Butler

My father, who had been a prisoner of war for three years, always had the same reply. "Father, you could have spared the world an awful lot of trouble, and saved my digestion, if you had borrowed a revolver and shot him." Father Butler always used to bridle at this, and muttered that shooting the man would have been taking the concept of the Church militant one step too far. He was a remarkable man, Father Butler, who was mourned by all when he finally departed this life at a very great age.

CHAPTER NINE

The south east and its treasurers

This chapter is devoted to some of the changes that Ireland's South East has witnessed. It is an unashamed plug for a world where I have a direct commercial interest. Leaving that aside, it does show how a real backwater in a country like Ireland can be transformed by the right initiatives taken by the authorities, backed up by a willing populace. It shows how the heritage of one part of Ireland can be developed, and made accessible to visitors from all over the world.

I was eleven years old in 1963, the year that President Kennedy was assassinated. At that time, to describe the South East as a cultural desert does not do justice to cultural deserts. There was nothing there. For sure, there was an agricultural economy, which had its ups and downs. Otherwise, there was no progress. The area seemed stuck in some kind of time warp. The idea that that part of Ireland might have a lot else to offer had not caught hold at all.

Times have changed. On the initiative of Failte Ireland, the County Councils, and organizations like the Kennedy Trust, the tourism potential has been developed to the point where it is really overtaking other less fortunate parts of Ireland.

As I have said, I have a direct commercial interest in this progress. I own a Cistercian monastery called Dunbrody Abbey. Some thirty years ago I decided to take the bull by the horns and start a tourist development at the Abbey. I have put in all the infrastructure that you might expect, such as adequate car parking. However, I did not think that the Abbey on its own would make a commercially viable business. I wanted to attract families on holiday in the summer months. The idea I hit on was to plant a hedge maze out of yew trees – this for the kids to get lost in, much to the joy of their parents. Around the maze we have a nine-hole, pitch-and-putt golf course, again aimed at families with children of all ages. That is enough of my plug. My point here is that I have been given significant help over the years, confirming what I said in the first paragraph.

I asked for, and received, a substantial start-up grant, under a plan called the Agri-tourism scheme. That was fine, but the real help came from two men in particular, some years later. The first was a man called Eddie Breen, who for many years was the Wexford County Manager. Some say that the County Managers are the men that really run Ireland. I would concur with that. The second was Larry O'Brien, who was a County Councillor, who made his name by saving a number of lives in the Herald of Free Enterprise disaster off Zeebrugge. Larry is a neighbour and a friend.

These two men bent over backwards to help my initiative get on its feet, and stay on its feet. They were particularly helpful when I needed help the most. That was around the time when the Irish economy collapsed like a

A view of the Abbey across the water. The water in question is the Campile Pill, which flows into Waterford Harbour.

The abbey from the cloisters

pack of cards in 2007-2008. People talk about fair-weather friends. These two officials were the precise opposite. I like to think that they recognized a genuine attempt to further tourism in Wexford, and to build a business which would have the capacity to provide some long-term employment. I believe their view has been justified.

On one occasion I found myself in Leinster House, discussing the situation at Dunbrody Abbey with three very senior officials indeed. They were Frank Shalvey, Head of the National Monuments Division in the Office of Public Works, Paul Kehoe, a Wexford TD, and at the time Government Chief Whip, and Brian Hayes, a minister in the Department

The nave of the main church in Dunbrody Abbey

of Finance in charge of the OPW. People say you should never speak to the monkey when you should be speaking to the organ-grinder. Well, here I was speaking to three very senior organ-grinders and not a monkey in sight.

I cannot stress too much, that, while people rightly vent their frustrations with government at all levels, it is possible to talk to people who really can make a difference, if you go about it the right way, and above all else you are patient. I have mentioned here a few top public officials, who were prepared to listen to what I had to say, and as a result provide tangible help. I thank them.

The cultural desert has been transformed in so many areas that I cannot list all the improvements, and the list that follows is far from exclusive. I will now touch on some of the attractions that the South East can boast of.

First of all, partly because they are my area of concern, there are the Abbeys. There are four main Abbeys (in ruins) in the South East. They are Dunbrody and Tintern, with the Colclough garden nearby, in Wexford. Then there is Jerpoint, and Duiske, in Kilkenny. These are all Cistercian Monasteries, the Cistercian order being an off-shoot of the older Benedictine Order of Monks. Founded mainly in the 12th century, often with Norman influence, they all became victims of Henry the Eighth and Thomas Cromwell, at the time of the dissolution of the monasteries. This is when the Abbey and the lands at Dunbrody came into my family's ownership.

Sir Osborne Etchingham, who was, one might say, a confidant of Thomas Cromwell, was rewarded for his efforts and loyalty to the monarch with the Abbey and what was then a very large amount of the accompanying land.

These Abbeys are all significant monastic sites. They have fascinating histories, and through the efforts of the OPW they are very well maintained. I have heard complaints regarding the OPW, normally to do with the slow pace that they work at. That may be true, but the quality of their work is of the highest standard, and they do look after Ireland's National Monuments in exemplary fashion.

I have mentioned the assassination of President John F Kennedy in 1963. One of Ireland's most famous sons, it could be argued that this tragic act has had more to do with the emergence of the South East as an area of interest than any other single event. The Kennedys came from Wexford. The President's great-grandfather, Patrick Kennedy, emigrated from Wexford to America in 1849.

He had been reared at Dunganstown, which is a townland, just south of New Ross.

The assassination was the catalyst for all sorts of initiatives which really set the ball rolling. The arrival of Kennedy money, which would probably not have happened had the President lived, prompted all sorts of developments. The John F Kennedy trust has been instrumental in much of this. Its primary achievement has been to build and make available to the public the Dunbrody Famine ship, which is moored in New Ross. This is a replica of a ship of that name, which transported thousands of emigrants to the States. The Kennedy name lives on in the area in the shape of the Kennedy Homestead, Patrick Kennedy's original home; and on a much larger scale, the JFK Arboretum. This is a magnificent Park on 250 hectares on Slieve Coillte, a hill near to Dunbrody Abbey. The arboretum is a fascinating collection of trees, some planted in forest plots, and is a haven of peace and tranquility.

Possibly the greatest success story in the South East's drive for recognition is the opening of the Hook lighthouse at the end of the Hook peninsula. This claims to be the world's oldest operational lighthouse, which is a claim that is probably unprovable one way or the other. Some years ago, it ceased to be a manned lighthouse, and modern technology has meant it is fully automated, and no doubt more efficient. The whole area has been developed as a visitor attraction with astonishing success. I do not quite understand this success. It is an unusual place, but there are plenty of them in the country. Maybe it is to do with the idea that there is nothing between the lighthouse and the Americas!

The lighthouse on the Hook is in danger

The Hook lighthouse on a stormy day.

of becoming a victim of its own success. The big problem is traffic. The road out to the lighthouse is simply not adequate for the huge flows of traffic that are now in evidence every day during the summer. Something must be done, but who will pay for it?

Looking further afield, we find the Irish National Heritage Park, just north of Wexford town, and to the south, Johnstown Castle, with its agricultural museum. Johnstown Castle was originally built for the Esmonde family, but has been in public ownership since the middle of the last century. It has recently benefited from a huge cash injection, and is one of the area's top attractions.

It is not all about Wexford. Kilkenny City boasts the magnificent Kilkenny Castle. Originally the seat of the Dukes and Earls of Ormond, it is now the property of the Kilkenny people, and has been since the last Ormond handed it over for a nominal sum. As a point of interest, the family name of the Ormond titles is Butler. This is the same name, and they are related, as the Butlers, otherwise the Earls of Carrick, who started Mount Juliet.

In Waterford the magnificent estates of Curraghmore, and Mount Congreve are examples of how the old Irish aristocracy lived. There are very few of these properties left, but here are two prime examples.

If you visit the South East of Ireland, it is quite possible to have your fill of gardens, abbeys and castles. There are quite a number. A rather sarcastic American visitor said to me one day after visiting Dunbrody Abbey, "If I

Ireland can be a strange place. This fine pillar with ball finial stands in splendid isolation far out on the Hook peninsula. Surprisingly, not only does it have no companion, but there is no house either. Possibly some grand project ran out of money in record time.

see another ruined building in this country, I will jump off the Cliffs of Moher". For those of a more active frame of mind, then I would suggest the rivers and racecourses of the area provide a suitable diversion.

Ireland is the home of the horse, and the South East has traditionally produced some of the very best. It is the home of some great country race tracks, also some of the most prestigious. You can race at Tramore in Waterford, Gowran Park in Kilkenny, and Wexford in that county. Heading slightly further north to Kildare, you can visit Punchestown, or Ireland's Ascot, on the Curragh. I have been to all these courses, and seen my cash gobbled up by the bookies, but I have had an awful lot of fun in the process.

I have mentioned the fishing opportunities in an earlier chapter, so I would just pose this question. What other part of the world of similar size can boast salmon rivers of the calibre of the Blackwater, the Suir, the Nore, the Barrow, and the Slaney? These are all big rivers with potentially large stocks of salmon. The fate of the Atlantic salmon is precarious, but recent governments have taken note. Commercial netting off the coast of Ireland has been banned since 2006.

Finally, I have a story of such little consequence that I hesitate to mention it. I like to annoy my friends with a poser. The question is this. Once in my life, I have been very badly bitten by a horse that earlier in its racing career won two Champion Hurdles at Cheltenham, and countless other top races. What was the horse's name, and what were the circumstances? The answer is as follows:-

A few years ago, I had a Polish cousin of

On the Hook Peninsula – Who on earth gave permission for such a monstrosity, and why has it not been demolished ?

mine, Marek Kwiatkowski, to stay. He was on an Irish tour, which he said he would find refreshing. He certainly did. I thought that I would take him to the Irish National Stud, which is near the Curragh in a village called Tully in Kildare. The stud is a wonderful advertisement for Irish bloodstock. I do not know whose idea it was, but some bright spark hit on the plan to put aside a couple of paddocks for use as a retirement home for some of Ireland's greatest horses when their racing days are done.

When we went on our guided tour of the stud, we visited these paddocks, as part of the tour. The guide set about introducing some of the retired stars to the assembled company.

Self lost in a maze of my own creation!

"There is Moscow Flyer. There is Kicking King. Oh, and over there, that's Beef or Salmon." – famous horses in their day. All of a sudden, a tiny horse, really no more than a pony, barged his way through the throng, spotted me leaning on the fence, made a lunge at me, grabbed my arm, and bit as hard as he could. His name was Hurricane Fly, and he was the best of the lot. He could certainly bite. I had the bruise for weeks.

The guide, rather unhelpfully, said to me, as I nursed my wounded arm. "I was just about to tell you about him. He's the boss man – no question."
"Thanks for the warning!" It was entirely my own fault for not paying attention.

Above: An unusual picture of the Abbey in the snow. It is quite rare to get a complete covering like this.

Opposite page: Another angle on the Maze. A great place to visit in the summer.

CHAPTER TEN
Words of caution

While the progress that has been made in this part of Ireland is astounding, and, at long last, a lot of important sites are available to the general public to visit, I would sound a few words of caution. It is all too easy to kill the goose that lays the golden egg. There are drawbacks and problems, such as the traffic on the Hook, but my main worry could be described like this.

There is a phrase that you hear in Ireland, and I have never heard it anywhere else. That phrase is "Cute Hoorism". As far as I know there is no formal dictionary definition of the word or words. To the uninitiated, what it means is a willingness to benefit from any given situation by sharp practice or in an underhand manner - the opposite of straight dealing.

The world of tourism throughout Ireland does suffer the odd outbreak of "Cute Hoorism". It is not that widespread, but it is there. I will give the reader one or two examples.

A few years ago, I took my family and a few friends on holiday to Mayo – quite close to Achill Island. We had a great time, but one day it rained all day, so we went shopping. I found a typical tourist-trap type shop, and found to my astonishment a minuscule pot of raspberry jam being sold for Euro 8.50. I bought it, simply to see what the jam was like. Well, it was no better or worse than any other jam. The exorbitant price was justified, I suppose, by the frilly ribbons which decorated the jar. Now that is an example of "Cute Hoorism".

There is still an enthusiasm for selling or attempting to sell figures of little green men, brandishing sticks. These represent leprechauns with their shillelaghs. This is tat. It always has been tat, and it always will be tat. Who wants to buy an ugly green man anyway?

On a larger scale, there is the perennial problem of overcharging for hotel accommodation, and hotel food. This is far from universal, but it does happen, and it gets the whole industry a bad name. I could name one or two. It is now standard practice to charge for admission to the many tourist attractions. These charges are normally reasonable, but not always. With Ireland entering a post-Covid world, there is no scope for price increases on admission charges, and particularly beds in hotels. Over the years I have spoken to thousands of foreign tourists at Dunbrody Abbey. Without a doubt the commonest complaint is the price of hotel accommodation, closely followed by the weather! We can do nothing about the latter, but the former needs attention. The prices are high enough. Don't kill that goose.

Another phrase you hear is "Rip-Off Ireland". Again the situation in the opinion of this observer is better than it was, but we must all work to see the back of "Cute Hoorism" and its close relation "Rip-Off Ireland". If we don't, then we will deserve what we get, which will not be much.

One final whinge, and it is a whinge, is the proliferation of government-backed schemes that get launched with a great fanfare, and then just get lost in the public sector morass. I am always left with the impression that there are too many cooks spoiling this particular broth. There is a limit to the number of glossy magazines produced at public expense that the average tourist can be expected to leaf through. Anyway, in these days of social media, all other methods of advertising are beginning to look of dubious value. How long before the traditional flyer is no more?

CHAPTER ELEVEN
Hope for the future

The last chapter dealt with some of the negatives, but what about the positives? There is so much to be positive about.

In this chapter I plan to have a look at some of those positives. I should stress that these are the opinions of someone who has entered his eighth decade. My views may well be seen as out of touch, but I have seen a fair bit of the world, and these views, which may upset some people, are genuinely held ones.

First of all, what does the post-Covid world hold in store for the South East of Ireland, and for the country as a whole? It may be, though I doubt it, and I fervently hope not, that large scale tourism with substantial numbers of foreign visitors is a thing of the past. If Covid proves to be impossible to eradicate, and mutates to a far more lethal strain, then all bets are off. The human race would be in a fight for survival, and the cost of a night in a Bed and Breakfast in Co. Kilkenny would be the least of anyone's worries.

Even in the best-case scenario, however, priorities are bound to change, and given that domestic tourism becomes the bread and butter of the industry, things will be very different in the years ahead from what we have become used to. I think Ireland is very well placed to deal with these changes and will continue to attract a fair number of foreign visitors. Here is why.

A few years ago, I had an old friend to stay in Wexford in order to shoot snipe. He happened to live in the English midlands. Rather late at night, we were putting the world to rights, and talking a lot of undiluted rubbish. In amongst the garbage, I do remember this.

I wondered out loud what it was that he most liked about Ireland. Expecting a reply of "snipe bogs" or "Irish racing", or "Guinness" or whatever, I was astonished to hear him say- "The best part about Ireland is that nobody lives here".

Setting aside the obviously non-sensical part of his comment, I believe he had a real point to make, and one that is easy to overlook. Just consider the following. The population density of these countries is as follows. The United Kingdom 275 people per square kilometre, France 122 per sq k, Holland 508 per sq k, and the Republic of Ireland just 72 per sq k. Relatively speaking nobody does live here. Put another way, the population density of the United Kingdom, including the wilds of Scotland, Wales, and the Pennines, is roughly four times that of Ireland. I find that a terrifying statistic.

If you accept, and most do, that nearly all the world's problems are attributable to over-population, then Ireland is in a uniquely benign position.

To back up my friend's assertion, I remember speaking to a charming Dutch couple in the car park at Dunbrody Abbey. They came from a small town a few miles east of Amsterdam. They were effusive about the delights of Ireland. "Why?" I asked. "Oh, that is easy to answer." they said in unison. "It is the wildness of the country. We don't have that in Holland".

A couple of years ago I drove over the hills from Mullinavat in Kilkenny to New Ross in Wexford. It was about 8 o'clock in the evening in February. I did not pass one single living soul on a trip of fifteen miles or so. There were no cars, no men on bikes, no pedestrians, no-one at all. The idea that you could do that anywhere in England is simply laughable.

In previous times, that dearth of people might well have been seen as a source of national shame. "Poverty and potato blight have stripped the country bare of all its people" might have been the cry. Not today. I believe the relatively low population is an absolutely priceless asset, which we will squander at our peril.

To preserve this low level of population, and what remains a largely unspoiled land, at least in comparison to some of our neighbours, Ireland will have to leave the European Union. Otherwise, it risks being swamped at the behest of Brussels. I ask this question; What self-respecting sovereign nation does not decide on its own immigration policy?

It has been an article of faith for many that membership of the European Union is an indisputable blessing. But is it? In very recent, times Brussels' real views on Ireland were laid bare, when it proved quite prepared to impose a hard border on the island of Ireland in an attempt to bring the United Kingdom into line on the question of vaccines. This drove a coach and horses through the Good Friday agreement, and demonstrated to all and sundry that their real interest in Ireland was that it provided them with a convenient stick with which to beat the British.

Just wait until they get going on Ireland's corporate tax rate. This stands at the moment at 12.5%, with the likes of Apple and Microsoft, the real multinationals, paying as little as 2.2% to 4.5% on global profits shifted to Ireland. The headline corporate tax rate in the UK is 19%, rising to 25% on 1st April 2023. The same rate in France is 28%. I do not see the European Union – which is dominated by Germany and France – tolerating that difference for too long. Since writing these lines corporate tax rates have moved centre stage with the G7 announcement. My views are already out of date.

I strongly suspect that Ireland's love affair with the European Union is doomed. If so, where does Ireland and Irish tourism go? What is the future?

Back to basics may well prove to be the answer. The country will have to capitalize on its principal assets. These are, among others, the fact that it is not overcrowded (yet), and has that quality that attracted the Dutch couple in abundance. It so happens that two of the country's chief assets are in just the areas that will attract the high value and high spending tourist or foreign investor that the country so badly needs.

Let us look first at the state of National Hunt racing in Ireland. At a recent Cheltenham festival meeting, I looked on in astonishment as Irish-trained horses won 23 out of the 28 races. I don't think it is clever to be triumphalist about this, and I do not think such total domination of the English horses by the Irish ones is a good thing for the sport. All the same, Ireland should capitalize on such success. I am not suggesting that it does not, but it can go further.

If you happen to be called Mr. Rich Ricci, and you have a very promising young hurdler on your hands, where are you going to send this star in the making to be trained? Why – Bagenalstown in Co. Carlow of course – the home of Mr. W. P. Mullins. Ireland will attract the big players in the world of horse ownership provided the likes of Willie Mullins keep the record they do have at all the big events. There is absolutely no sign of the current dominance of the Irish coming to an end.

Talking of the Mullins family, my father told me an amusing story about Paddy Mullins, who was Willie's father. Paddy was a great man, and a great trainer. In fact, he was a top man all round. His best horse by a mile was that incomparable mare Dawn Run.

I was determined to get him in somewhere, and so I have. Johnny Harrington with his own winner at Punchestown. He made a huge contribution to racing and life in general in the South-East. Here he is with the Harrington team, sporting a broad grin. The grin seemed to be permanent.

Thady Dunraven, brother of Melissa Brooke, and Caroline Waterford. He contracted polio at an early age, and was wheelchair-bound for the rest of his life. It did not stop him from enjoying his racing.

Dawn Run's owner was a lady from Waterford called Charmian Hill. Mrs Hill had a reputation, and this is being polite, for her parsimony. She was not given to splashing the cash in any circumstances.

After one of Dawn Run's triumphs at Cheltenham, Paddy thought that it was high time that the mare's owner put her hand in her pocket and gave the lads in the Mullins yard a present. He suggested this to Mrs. Hill, who thought for a moment and then agreed that she would bring a present for them on her next visit.

The great day arrived, and Mrs. Hill came with her present, which was

Two champions taking it easy at Commonstown. Alpha Centauri with Debbie Flavin up is on the left. Sizing John with Kate Harrington up is on the right. It must be highly unusual to find a Coronation Stakes winner at Royal Ascot passing the time of day with a Cheltenham Gold Cup winner.

not in bulging brown envelopes as Paddy had expected. It was in a biscuit tin. She proudly opened the tin for Paddy to inspect the contents. It was a fruit cake which appeared to have been paid a visit by a family of mice. "I have brought the lads a present. I hope they enjoy it", said Mrs. Hill.

The story goes that Paddy Mullins was so embarrassed that he gave the lads a cash present out of his own pocket, as if it had come from Mrs. Hill. Not knowing what to do with the fruit cake, he ate it himself for his tea!

Any rich owner, normally not bothered by fruitcakes, is unlikely to look any further for a trainer than one of the top Irish ones. Willie Mullins, Henry de Bromhead, Jessica Harrington, or, provided he becomes camera shy, Gordon Elliot. These are the people who can do wonders for the country, and its foreign earnings. Of course, that is before one even thinks of the Coolmore and the world of the flat. It is just that the superiority of the Irish over the English is more marked in the National Hunt world. Ireland's astonishing success is hard to explain. I certainly can't, but success

Two winning ladies. Alpha Centauri with her trainer, after winning the Coronation stakes in 2018.

breeds success, and long may it continue.

Next, we have the rivers, and the huge potential of all forms of game fishing. Here the benefit of a low population and hopefully manageable levels of pollution has to be an ace in the pack for Ireland. In recent times I have spent some of the year living close to the river Tweed in Scotland (though part of the river flows through England). It is a wonderful river, the most prolific fly water in Britain. There is one serious drawback to my mind. It is scandalously over-fished. On a day a few years ago, I was fishing with a friend, when we realized that we were in competition with four other rods who were all in plain view, and all within 400 yards of each other. We packed up and went home. Too many people are the problem.

Ireland has the luxury of enough river mileage of fishable water, and the scope to avoid this over-fishing problem, provided there is a will to eschew the quick buck. I know there are very many well-heeled fishermen who would pay a handsome premium to fish somewhere (anywhere), with no other rod in view, on water that they knew had not been thrashed to a foam the day before. You could call it quality rather than quantity.

In an earlier chapter, I mentioned the fishing at Mount Juliet in the time of Major Dermot McCalmont. Such largesse as he displayed is no longer possible. I accept that. But I am sure a less commercial approach would pay dividends, not just in respect of the catches, but in respect of the people doing the catching. Ireland should try harder to attract people who can push cash into other aspects of the economy, and, yes, I am talking of the Mr. Rich Riccis of the fishing world. There are plenty of them. It is a fact that one Mr. Ricci is worth more to the Irish economy than hundreds of German and French tourists in their camper wagons. They probably bring their Bratwurst and Camembert with them. They are self-contained and tend to spend little in the country.

As a part of the plan for superior fishing in Ireland more attention should be paid to care of the spawning beds, and, crucially, the improvement of water quality. Sadly, there are still too many instances of silage effluent and the like escaping into water-courses with a devastating impact on the fry and parr populations of these waters. The Government cannot control what happens off Greenland but it certainly can in the area west of Athy!

One other huge change that is coming is the nature of holiday accommodation. Coming into its own will be the self-catering cottage. It already has, but the scope for growth is considerable. It seems certain that in the future the avoidance of disease will be paramount, therefore the holiday cottage will score heavily over the hotel and even the B and B, where you cannot guarantee the health status of others, or that regularly used surfaces have been disinfected.

Caravan parks, mobile homes, and even tents will become much more popular, if things work out as I expect. As for the traditional pub, I am afraid the future may be very bleak indeed.

The final positive I propose to look at is, in my view, the most exciting of them all. If you ask yourself the question what form of activity will people turn to that is more or less disease free, does not harm the planet, and cures society of some of its ills (notably obesity) then the answer must be walking and running in all their different guises. I have not even mentioned golf.

Springing up all over Ireland, and certainly in the South East, are the Greenways and walking trails. To deal with the Greenways first. Five years ago, on a holiday to Mayo, most of our rather large party went to try out the Great Western Greenway between Westport and Achill island, passing along the shores of Clew Bay. They hired bikes at a very reasonable cost. The bikes were all in good condition, and the party had a wonderful day. They came back exhausted and weather-beaten, but delighted with themselves. According to them the Greenway was packed with people having a similarly good time. No cars, no exhaust fumes, no conditions suitable for the transmission of Covid or anything else unpleasant, what is there to complain about?

There is a Greenway planned between New Ross and Waterford City, and another between Waterford and Rosslare. I look forward to these being fully functional. To declare my hand, the Rosslare version, if approved, would pass no more than 100 yards from Dunbrody Abbey. I, and others will look to benefit, and why not?

Finally, there is the concept of the Coastal Trail. There are plenty up and running in Ireland, but coastal trails seem to have been a more recent development in the South East.

To put my money where my mouth is, in a manner of speaking, I have recently given the green light to the creation of a coastal trail through Dunbrody Park. This connects the villages of Arthurstown and Duncannon. It is stunning. The views of Waterford harbour are breathtaking.

I say this only half in jest. One of the great views in Ireland may become the sight of the top of the bald head of a container ship Captain, as he navigates his marine monster on its way up river. It is a peculiar feature of the channel in the estuary that it has carved a path very close to the cliff in Dunbrody Park. The visual effect is that some huge ships seem within touching distance. That bald head will be a great photo opportunity!

EPILOGUE

That describes the *"Heaven on Earth"*, which my sister, Chich, referred to. It was a wonderful but undiscovered part of Ireland. It has changed, and the players on the stage are a very different type today. When I was a boy, this part of the country was a playground for some outlandish characters, who might not have been able to survive in 21st century Ireland. Humour and the horse dictated much of their lives. It just leaves me to ask the question. "What has happened to the old Anglo-Irish families, who were having their last throw of the dice in the 1950s and 1960s?"

Surprisingly, to some, while most have gone to the four winds, there is fight in that particular dog yet. After all, it is not the size of the dog in the fight that matters, but the size of the fight in the dog.

For sure, it is a different sort of aristocracy that rules the roost throughout Ireland today. It might be better described as a plutocracy, willingly supported by an overweight bureaucracy. The new money billionaires have taken over, but even their power is illusory. The real power resides in Brussels, not in Dublin at all.

Whatever your views on the European Union, whether you like it or loathe it, and I am firmly in the latter camp, no Irishman ever voted to be run by the faceless functionaries of the Berlaymont. It is the ultimate irony for me, that one hundred years after the Republic gained its sovereignty from Westminster, it has given that sovereignty away again, but to a different foreign power. Why? Just for the money? If so, then the country is in for a shock.

As I say, the remnants of the families I knew so well are putting up quite a fight against the ravages of time. There is no chance that the Ireland I grew up in can ever return. It has gone forever, but here are some examples of the survivors' achievements.

Chich, my sister, was married to John Fowler of Rahinston Co. Meath. John was a successful amateur jockey, till the weight got the better of him. The real star turn of that family has been John's sister Jessie Harrington. She has become one of Ireland's most successful trainers. She trains on the flat, and over the jumps, at Commonstown, just outside Moone, in Co. Kildare. In her career she has trained a number of horses who have been household names. Among the best are the following:- Sizing John, Moscow Flyer, Jezki, and Alpha Centauri. There are many more.

Still in the world of racing, I have already touched on Harry McCalmont's success in the breeding game. He has turned the Norelands stud into a great story. Near to me in Wexford, Patrick Berridge ran, for many years, a successful cheese-making company. Carrigbyrne cheese is not to be missed.

On a different scale altogether, Ambrose Congreve of Mount Congreve on the Suir, just up the river from Waterford City, had a hugely successful career as an industrialist, running, and eventually owning, Humphreys and Glasgow, a company set up in the field of marine engineering by his father-in-law, Doctor Arthur Glasgow. Ambrose died in 2011, aged 104. No-one knows just how much money he made in the second half of the 20th century, but it was a lot, his enduring legacy being the magnificent garden at Mount Congreve. Ambrose was a controversial character, who resembled some kind of latter-day buccaneer, but he was one of life's great achievers.

Johnny Price's old home, Kilmokea Gardens, was bought in the 1990s by Mark and Emma Hewlett. They have turned a property which was fraying at the edges, into one of the real gems of the South East. When my son James got married, I put up family and friends at Kilmokea. It was wonderful. A number of the guests, when they wrote to me after the event, said that they wanted to go back, just for the pleasure of staying there. What is more the tariff is quite fair. The gardens are lovely, and the atmosphere near perfect. What could be better?

I hope I have given the reader a flavour of what this part of Ireland was like fifty years ago. At times it seemed like a mad house, but it was and still is a real heaven on earth.

Kilmokea in all its summer glory.

BY THE SAME AUTHOR
The 4th Lord Templemore

Claud Chichester, the 4th Baron Templemore was the author's grandfather. He was a typical representative of the Anglo-Irish landowning families.

Born at the height of empire, his motto, if he had one, could have been "For family. king, and country". He was scrupulously loyal to all three. Here is an account of his life, a life devoted to those three entities, even if it was not always clear which country he had in mind. He seems to have loved England and Ireland equally, often a precarious position to hold.

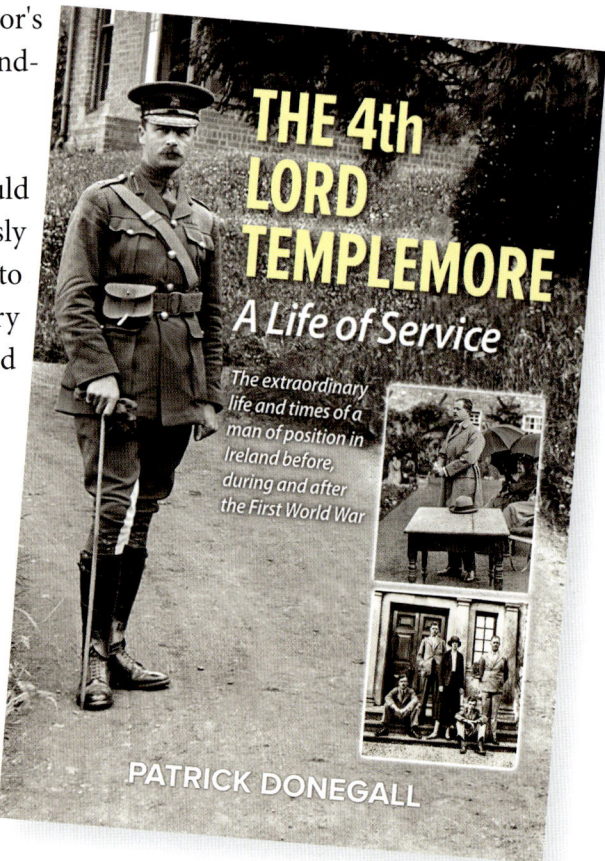

CONTENTS
Forward
1   Claud's Background
2   The Early Years
3   Life in the Fusiliers
4   The Tibet Expedition of 1904
5   Peacetime soldiering, The Isle of Wight and Ireland
6   Marriage and a Political Baptism
7   Northern Ireland and the Ulster Crisis
8   1914-1918 War. Irish Guards and the Staff
9   Between the Wars and Claud's succession to the peerage
    The 1930s and the 1939-1945 War
10 The Final Years
11 Claud's Legacy
12 Acknowledgements

St Edward's Press Ltd
20 Barra Close, Highworth, Wilts, SN67HX.
Email: info@stedwardspress.co.uk. Phone 01793 762417
www.stedwardspress.co.uk

ISBN 978-1-909650-17-6
Published – 1 March 2020
2nd Edition – 1 December 2020
Format – 210 x 148 mm
Binding – Paperback
Pages – 107
Illustrations – Fifty-five

Price £10
(£12 including UK post.)

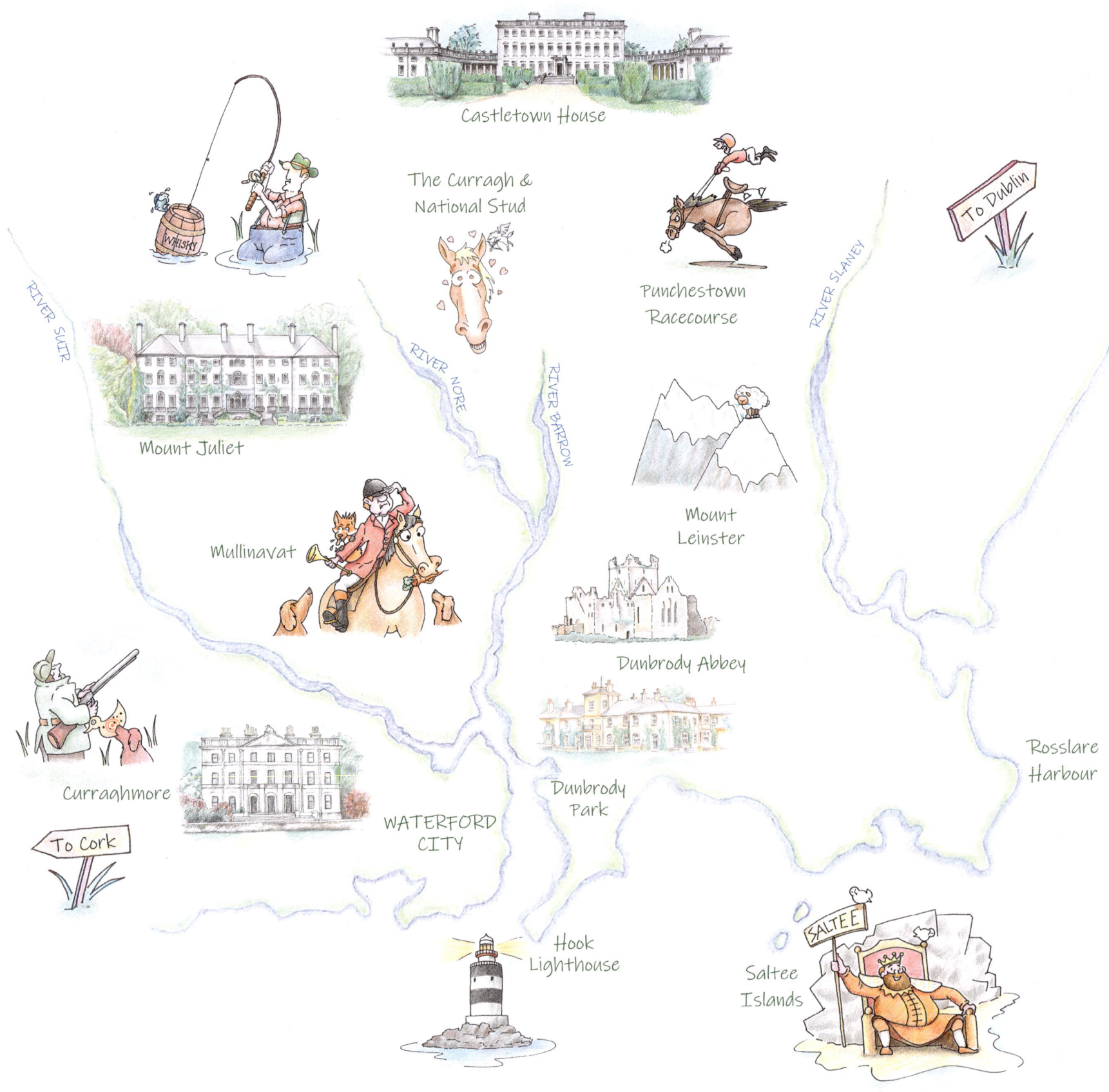